Metaphors of English body-part words and collocations

Daniel Aberra

Metaphors of English body-part words and collocations

Daniel Aberra

Metaphors of English body-part words and collocations

Daniel Aberra

Contents

Introduction

In the 2010s, the Linguistics Department in the University of Alberta was a hub of groundbreaking research in cognitive-corpus linguistics, child language acquisition, mental lexicon, and the sound sciences. The Department hosted a web of world-renowned linguists in these areas and gave students chances to rub shoulders. While we, the students, caught up in the frenzy that was going on in the Department, some of us went off the grid from our goals for one or the other reasons. Still, I believe we all have benefitted from the frenzy. This book, metaphors of English body-part words and collocations, is one of the benefits.

In one of the lectures at the Department, John Newman has discussed collocations of body-part words. He concluded that body part words fluctuate in meaning based on their frequent co-occurrences with other words and their various conjugations. Who may think of 'a hand' versus 'hands' distinction, that a hand is used to put on someone's knee but "hands-on (one's own) knees" or hands to hold one's face? Who may have thought of a "hand-on knee" versus "hands-on (one's own) hip(s)"?

These extensive usages of everyday anthropomorphic and zoomorphic body part words fascinate me. Hence, whenever I read the North American news in digital and social media and come across body-part words in contexts with different metaphorical meanings, I have collected them. In this book you will find the result of this decade-old collection. This book compiles the 1000 authentic examples of body-part anthropomorphic and zoomorphic words and their metaphorical meanings.

The body-part entries are classified alphabetically from A-Z under the 129 body-part head-words. Then the 1000 expressions, i.e., collocations of the head-words, have been listed followed by their metaphorical definitions. Authentic, metaphorical usages of the English body-part words follow the definitions. The sources of the authentic examples have been listed last.

The authentic expressions have been collected from about fifty different North American digital and social media sources, of which 12.7% are Canadian, and 87.4% are from the US.

I got help from several people; some have to be mentioned by name, my spouse Yemesrach, my sons Nebiy and Dagmawi and family members Haileleul and Dereje. Thank you all!

I invite you all to flip the book's pages and reflect on the phrase "skin in the game" and recall the "Radiohead" band and the "earmark" budgeting of the American congress to that of "chaps my hide". I hope you will have an amazing journey!

DA 2021

Abbreviations and the source pages

ABC = http://blogs.abcnews.com/

BC   =   http://www.boston.com/

BLM =   http://www.bloomberg.com/

CA   =   https://pressprogress.ca/

CAAB =   Change Alberta Face book page

CABDC = https://www.bdc.ca/

CAGLB = https://globalnews.ca/

CANBA = https://ca.nba.com/

CANP =   https://nationalpost.com

CAYA =   https://ca.news.yahoo.com/

CAYYG = http://www.calgaryherald.com/n

CB   =   http://cavett.blogs.nytimes.com/

CBC =   http://www.cbc.ca/

CBS =   http://www.cbsnews.com/

CNN =   http://www.cnn.com/

CTCC =   https://toronto.ctvnews.ca/

DK   =   http://www.dailykos.com/

DMC =   http://www.dickmorris.com/

DMUK = http://www.dailymail.co.uk/

EB   =   http://embeds.blogs.foxnews.com/

FC   =   http://www.freep.com/

GGL =   https://www.google.com/

HB   =   http://hardblogger.msnbc.msn.com

HEC =   http://www.humanevents.com/

HP   =   http://www.huffingtonpost.com/

KC   =   http://kossacksnetworking.ning.com/

MN   =   http://minnesotaindependent.com/

MSN =   http://www.msnbc.msn.com/

MWC =   http://apnews.myway.com/
MYDD =   http://www.mydd.com/
NA =   https://www.huffpost.com/
NEWSY = http://news.yahoo.com/
NWC =   http://www.newsweek.com/
NYB =   https://www.nybooks.com/
NYD =   https://www.nydailynews.com/
NYDC =   http://www.nydailynews.com/
NYNC =   http://www.nydailynews.com/
NYTC =   http://www.nytimes.com/
OC =   http://blogs.orlandosentinel.com/
PC =   http://www.politico.com/
REU =   http://www.reuters.com/
RSC =   http://www.redstate.com/
SFGC =   http://www.sfgate.com/
STBC =   https://susanonthesoapbox.com/
STSB =   https://susanonthesoapbox.com/
SYPC =   http://steveyoungonpolitics.com/
TBC =   https://www.thefreelibrary.com/
TC =   https://twitter.com/
TGC =   https://www.theguardian.com/
TOUK =   http://www.timesonline.co.uk/
TSC =   https://www.thestar.com/
TTC =   https://www.thestar.com/
TWT =   https://twitter.com/
WP =   http://www.washingtonpost.com/
YEG =   http://edmontonjournal.com/

Head words

anal

anal retentive — (of a person) excessively orderly and fussy Eg."I know 650 anal retentive patriots."[DK]

ankle

to ankle (out) — to walk away from one's employment; ~ to leave Eg."Hillary is probably ready to ankle out of the Senate."[NYTC]

grab our ankles — to seize hold of (something); ~ to seize illegally or unscrupulously; ~ to arrest; ~ catch; ~ (of a brake or clutch in a vehicle) to grip and release intermittently causing juddering Eg."We are being told we have to hope he succeeds, that we have to grab our ankles."[SFGC]

arm

arm in arm — closely allied, intimate; ~ (of two or more people) with arms linked Eg."I think we can only endure if we pull together and do it arm in arm."[DK]

arm's length — a distance discouraging personal contact or familiarity; ~ the condition or fact that the parties to a transaction are independent and on an equal footing Eg."The arm's length approach was the administration's latest attempt to strike."[MSN]

break their arms — to excessively praise for an achievement or a job well done Eg."You can't break their arms, you can't put your whole relationship on the line."[PC]

lock arms — join arms tightly with the arms of the people on each side Eg."If these pro lifers are so pro life, then maybe they should lock arms and block cemeteries."[DK]

off arms — to talk to one for such a long time that one becomes exhausted or bored Eg."Banks could have worked with people on their loans and taken people off arms."[DK]

open arms — an eager or warm welcome Eg."We welcome you back with opened arms and big hugs! "[DK]

opened his arms — an eager or warm welcome Eg."Obama opened his arms wide when he spotted his secretary of state, Hillary Rodham Clinton."[HP]

powerful arm — using or characterized by force or violence; ~ use force or violence against Eg."Financial Sector (which includes insurance) is now the most powerful arm inside the government."[DK]

Sergeant-at-Arms — serves as the executive officer of the legislative assembly for enforcement of rules Eg."Briefly, they made a sandwich of Senate Sergeant-at-Arms Terrance Gainer, who scooted out from between them."[HP]

to arms — a summons to engage in active hostilities; ~ a summons, invitation, or appeal to undertake a particular course of action a political call to arms Eg."Then he'd ask the people to call their congress people to express their wishes, and to arms to get his back."[DK]

twist arms — to try to force someone to do something Eg."If big health can twist their arms, why can't we? "[DK]

up in arms — protesting vigorously about something; ~ to be very angry Eg."He is so up in arms about Rand Paul being a racist. I'm not up in arms about him being racist."[DK]

up in arms — protesting vigorously about something; ~ to be very angry Eg."CBN's David Brody that anti-abortion groups are up in arms over Kansas Gov. Kathleen Sebelius potentially leading HHS."[MSN]

arm bar

arm bar — a submission maneuver designed to hyper extend the elbow joint forcing an opponent to tap out. could be found in Eg."I knew I was supposed to get an arm bar on him, but he got me on the spin move with the and-1."[MSN]

armpit

armpits — a place regarded as extremely unpleasant Eg."You can't see his armpits."[HP]

ass

ass off — very hard; ~ to emphasize the activity as having been done to the maximum degree Eg."That didn't stop him from working his ass off to get through college."[DK]

asses — to behave stupidly and look silly Eg."Many lawmakers responded by voting no, worried about saving their asses in the election."[DK]

asses off — very hard; ~ to emphasize the activity as having been done to the maximum degree Eg."We just need to keep working our asses off to make it happen."[DK]

badass — (a) tough, uncompromising, or intimidating person Eg."This is some badass road clearing."[DK]

bet your ass — one can be very certain of something Eg."I am not of the age nor of a medical profile to need these medications but you can bet your ass that if I were..."[DK]

big ass — very large, expansive, fat, impressive, muscular, intimidating, or important quotations Eg."Oh yeah, he had to ditch those big-ass 80s glasses he used to wear."[HP]

cover one's ass — foresee and avoid the possibility of attack or criticism Eg."I wish he'd admit to his mistakes instead of always trying to cover his ass."[GGL]

dumb ass — (a) stupid or contemptible (person) Eg."One can be college educated and still be a dumb ass."[DK]

dumb ass — (a) stupid or contemptible (person) Eg."Do not let some dumb ass talk about freaking death panels."[DK]

gavel up his ass — to give a violent push Eg. "personally shove his committee gavel up his ass and pull it out through his nose."[DK]

kick ass — strikingly or overwhelmingly tough, aggressive, powerful, or effective Eg."She doesn't have to do anything to get re-elected, but she kicks ass."[DK]

kick ass — strikingly or overwhelmingly tough, aggressive, powerful, or effective Eg."We just have to kick ass continually."[DK]

kick his ass — strikingly or overwhelmingly tough, aggressive, powerful, or effective Eg."Diaries around here were howling that he was weak, and letting McCain kick his ass."[DK]

my ass — used to convey that one does not believe something that has just been said Eg."Conservatives can bite my ass, the hateful, nonproductive, divisive, bigots that they are."[DK]

my ass — used to convey that one does not believe something that has just been said Eg."Compare that statement to Obama's. Country first, my ass ..."[DK]

my ass — used to convey that one does not believe something that has just been said Eg."I would bet my hat/my ass/my shoes they don't show up. Pay attention."[DK]

off my ass — to stop bothering someone about something (often used as an order) Eg."Also, me brake checking you 3 times means get the f*** off my ass."[TC]

out of her ass — to say foolish things; ~ to talk of nonsense; ~ to exaggerate one's achievements or knowledge of some subject; ~ to bluff or boast Eg."Maybe she pulled some stuff right out of her ass, and he didn't have anything prepared to counter it" [DK]

smart ass — a person who is irritating because they behave as if they know everything Eg."Basically, I have two speeds.... Hostile or smart-ass. Your choice."[DK]

ass - shit

shit out of their ass — to physically attack one, as with punches and other blows, such that they suffer significant injury Eg."Well, guess what, they're pull this shit out of their ass."[DK]

asshole

asshole — a stupid, irritating, or contemptible person Eg."He did absolutely destroy those pretentious assholes."[DK]

asshole — a stupid, irritating, or contemptible person Eg."He knows Limbaugh may be an asshole but he is no fool."[DK]

asshole — a stupid, irritating, or contemptible person Eg."He's just a jerk. A debutante, status quo asshole with a big mouth and an ego to match."[DK]

assholes — stupid, irritating, or contemptible persons Eg."Pass HCR because excuses are like assholes, everybody has one."[DK]

back

back down — withdraw a claim or assertion in the face of opposition Eg."Yesterday, he didn't back down on his plans to change health care when he spoke on a radio program."[DK]

back of him/ her — you are pleased that you no longer have to be involved with him, her Eg."But now, as the Brits say, "I'll be glad to see the back of her."[CB]

back to back — consecutive, consecutively, in succession Eg."Can't do it all back to back without a few pauses in between the action."[DK]

back up your thinking — supply evidence, to support (a fact or opinion) by giving proof Eg."Let's see something to back up your thinking."[DK]

backbreaker — an extremely arduous task Eg."Stunning goal. A total backbreaker by Burrows."[CBC]

backfire — (of a plan or action) rebound adversely on the originator; ~ have the opposite effect to what was intended Eg. "and now it may just continue to backfire even more..."[DK]

backslap — to display excessive or effusive cordiality or goodwill Eg."Kerry's backslap marked McCain's induction into an unofficial bipartisan caucus."[HP]

backslappers — someone who's overly excited about congratulating you Eg."Fresh on the heels of Joe Lieberman's resounding re-acceptance into the Senate's secret club of back slappers... "[DK]

backstabbing — one who attacks or betrays someone in a deceitful, underhanded, or treacherous way Eg. "the media world of backstabbing, scheming, and downright malice "[GGL]

bareback — relating to or denoting sexual intercourse that is performed without a condom Eg."Can you believe that guy wanted to do it bareback? "[GGL]

fallback — an alternative plan that may be used in an emergency; ~ a reduction or retreat Eg."I absolutely think they'll have to have a fallback position."[DK]

to get someone's back — to be willing and prepared to help or defend someone; ~ to look out for someone in case they need assistance Eg."Then he'd ask the people to call their congress people to express their wishes, and to arms to get his back."[DK]

turn their backs on — you ignore them, leave them, or reject them Eg.“poorer Americans who have had their own American Congress turn their backs on ”[DK]

walk on my back — to retreat from or distance oneself from (a previously stated opinion or position) Eg.“Maybe I can just get somebody to walk on my back.”[DK]

watch my back — protect against danger from an unexpected quarter Eg.“if I'm Clarence I would watch my back, the president does not like him.”[MSN]

ball

break some balls — to seriously irritate or nag someone, to tease or ridicule someone Eg.“I include the president, who really needs to how to channel LBJ and start breaking some balls all ready.”[DK]

balls

by the balls — to have complete control or dominance over someone Eg.“Murdock needs to be executed, preferably by being hung by the balls.”[DK]

had the balls — had the courage Eg.“But if 100 million public option enthusiasts had the balls you do this thing would be a done deal.”[DK]

have the balls — have the courage Eg.“Our biggest problem is that we don't have the balls to stand firm on this.”[DK]

have the balls — have the courage Eg."He doesn't have the balls to stage this coup."[DK]

belly

belly laughs — a loud unrestrained laugh Eg."I give credit to Biden for not busting out in a fit of belly laughs right then and there."[DK]

belly of the beast — being in the middle of a very bad situation or a dangerous place Eg."She has chosen to venture into the belly of the beast."[PC]

belly up — a business, organization, or institution that has ceased to exist or gone bankrupt Eg."But she and her husband managed to sell their house just before the real estate market went belly up here in Los Angeles."[DK]

his bellicose ego — having an aggressive or fighting attitude/ ego Eg."to the benefit of massaging his bellicose ego and raking in great riches "[DK]

bile

bile — anger; ~ irritability Eg."they have all sorts of places in social media where they can express their bile "[CAAB]

bile-infused — anger; ~ irritability Eg."And they regurgitate all the chunky bile-infused horse crap."[DK]

bleed

bleeding — show sympathy, or express annoyance Eg."According to most of the pundits, Sarah stopped the bleeding."[DK]

bleeds — drains; ~ show sympathy Eg."Some of metropolitan Chicago bleeds over into IN."[DK]

bleeds to death last — to die;~ to lose last Eg."It's a case of he who bleeds to death last, wins."[FB]

is bleeding — show sympathy, or express annoyance Eg."Every day, popularity is bleeding and people are dying by spreadsheet."[DK]

blew

blew me away — are very impressed by it; ~ impressive Eg."He said the reception Monday from the fans "blew me away" and "touched my heart." "[MSN]

blink

blinked — got something difficult to handle Eg."In the end, he blinked and Obama did not… "[HP]

blinking first — whoever blinks first loses in an adult context, it sometimes refers to a hi-tension stand-off between fierce rivals Eg."He will been seen as blinking first… "[HP]

blood

bad blood — ill feeling Eg."She induced her old colleague John Kerry—despite some bad blood over his endorsement of Obama."[NWC]

blood flowing — let it get started; ~ move smooth as planned Eg."My guess is that plasma units are rushing to the McCain campaign as we speak to replace the blood flowing there from the fights among the staff."[HP]

blood sport — a violent sport or contest (such as hunting or cockfighting) involving bloodshed Eg."Politics is a blood sport."[NA]

blood sucking — a person who sponges or preys on another Eg."The blood sucking aristocracy stood aghast ... "[DK]

bloody — involving or characterized by cruelty or bloodshed Eg."Contemporary politics is a bloody battleground between real persons."[DK]

bloody murder — in a loud and violent manner ran off, screaming Eg."then once it was in force screamed bloody murder to get menthol banned ASAP "[DK]

bloodying — harming, damaging Eg."He'll be hit with the third-degree misdemeanor charge for allegedly bloodying Jack."[HP]

bucket of blood — an exclamation of frustration or surprise Eg."Craig MacTavish, lead hand in the bucket of blood operation that is Oilers senior management."[CAYEG]

go to be bloody — involving or characterized by cruelty or bloodshed Eg."But it is going to be bloody if Obama goes with 50."[DK]

 my blood bubble — warm up, heart warming Eg."She was totally full of it. I could tell 'cause my blood began to bubble."[DK]

new blood — new members admitted to a group, especially as an invigorating force Eg."Local governments are off to a good start, and may even manage to turn the infusion of new (or returning) blood to their advantage."[NWC]

out for blood — very angry and want to cause harm, pain or discomfort Eg."The Bruins were out for blood."[CBC]

returning blood — veterans, experienced members of the group Eg."local governments are off to a good start, and may even manage to turn the infusion of new (or returning) blood to their advantage "[NWC]

smelled blood — to recognize an opportunity to take advantage of someone who Is in a difficult situation Eg."And Pat Toomey, a conservative and former congressman who narrowly lost to Mr. Specter in the 2004 primary, smelled blood."[NYTC]

swear by the blood — a very serious or solemn oath Eg."Let every American... swear by the blood of the Revolution, never to violate ...the laws ..."[DK]

there's blood — worst off; ~ better opportunity to profit Eg."There's blood all over my hands in this, MacTavish said "[CAYEG]

blood-sweat-tears

blood, sweat and tears of — it is a very hard thing to do and requires a lot of effort Eg."I just barely helped out compared to the time, money, blood, sweat and tears of so many other people."[NEWSY]

body

body of work — the total output of a writer or artist (or a substantial part of it) Eg."But the freshly fired Eakins' body of work does not justify his former boss's kind words."[CAYEG]

body — the main section of Eg."And, you can body him a little. What do you know? Apparently it's better to get into Chara's grill."[CBC]

body — the main section of Eg."The heart will have stopped pumping blood to all extremities of the body economic."[DK]

embody — be an expression of or give a tangible or visible form to (an idea, quality, or feeling); ~ include or contain (something) as a constituent part Eg."Now, it's the Democrats who embody those values."[DK]

main body — main building blocks, backbone of some structure; ~ in academic writing where you deliver your argument Eg."Mental health issues face will be shoved aside from the main body of health treatments."[CAYEG]

bone

backbone — the chief support of a system or organization; ~ the mainstay Eg."Most of these individuals are really happy that at least he's showing some backbone."[PC]

bone to pick — having a grievance that needs to be talked out Eg."None of them dislike McCain, or have any bone to pick with Steve Schmidt or Rick Davis."[HP]

boned with — (of a person) having bones of the specified type; ~ (of meat or fish) having had the bones removed before cooking or serving Eg."Of course the immigrants are wealthier. They haven't been boned with the highest tax rates all of their lives."[CAYA]

boner — one that bones; ~ a clumsy or stupid mistake Eg."A boner is a terrible thing to waste."[DK]

raw boned — describing a person as being thin and bony, rugged but not necessarily handsome Eg."Scarborough slipped Monday while attempting to describe the rawboned manner of Rahm."[DK]

boot

give someone the boot — dismiss, fire someone from the job Eg."Give her the boot but it ain't enough to vote Liberal."[CBC]

brain

brain — referring to having intellectual capacity Eg."her brain is so good at spinning things into a comfortable fantasy "[DK]

brained — to strike or assault someone violently and severely, typically on the head Eg."The lump on my head is from when a box fell off a shelf and brained me yesterday."[GGL]

brain dead — irreversible cessation of all functions of the entire brain Eg."Atlee Williams[cop] have we become so brain dead that so many people are still voting for these morons, and some refuse to listen to the truth."[CAAB]

brain dead — irreversible cessation of all functions of the entire brain Eg."Free-market worshipping right wing and their legions of brain dead yet admirably loyal followers was nothing new."[DK]

brain dead — irreversible cessation of all functions of the entire brain Eg."Do you really think the brain-dead MSM would have focused at all."[DK]

brain goes in lockdown — being more forgetful than normal, can't plan or make decisions, being quick tempered Eg."Rand's brain goes into lockdown."[DK]

brain hurt — a sort of mental or emotional fatigue Eg."She makes my brain hurt! "[DK]

brain works — the effort of thought, reasoning, planning, or the like; ~ ordered or directed thinking Eg."I like you but I don't understand how your brain works... "[DK]

brainwash — make (someone) adopt radically different beliefs by using systematic and often forcible pressure Eg."From Men In Black to erase the memories of all the Americans she helped to brainwash with her lies and misinformation."[DK]

burnt in brain — displaying the adverse effects of drug use, especially cognitive impairment Eg."It was burnt in my brain."[YEG]

his brain wears — that it requires a lot of energy and makes you feel mentally or physically tired Eg."His brain wears gigantic puffy shoes and comes with a bicycle horn."[DK]

no brainer — something that requires or involves little or no mental effort Eg."It was a no-brainer," says Baisden, 45, whose freewheeling show reaches millions."[NWC]

working brain — work or effort consisting principally or largely of mental activity, thought, imagination, etc Eg."Anyone with a working brain easily saw through her BS."[DK]

breath

hold your breath — be in a state of suspense or anticipation Eg."When does he do an interview with Rachel or Ed? Don't hold your breath, base."[DK]

your breath — to wait for something specific to happen Eg."Don't waste your breath."[DK]

breeze

stiff breeze — talking rubbish Eg."Tiger actually radiated warmth to fans, when in the past they were goose-bumped from the stiff breeze as he blew by them."[MSN]

bum

bums — a vagrant Eg."Throw the bums out!" [DK]

butt

butt in — interrupt or intrude on a conversation or activity Eg."Sorry to butt in, but this poll needs your help."[DK]

butt-covering — foresee and avoid the possibility of attack or criticism Eg."while allowing butt-covering Senate Blue Dogs to shout "no" in the crowded theater ... "[DK]

butting heads — engage in conflict or be in strong disagreement Eg."The most popular theory places him on the Fox network, butting heads nightly with Letterman and Leno."[HP]

butts off — to work excessively hard Eg."I've noticed that most of the children of Asian immigrants are working their butts off in school."[CAYA]

fire his butt now — to stimulate, motivate someone to work or act more quickly Eg."What do I have to do "light a fire under your ass/ butt" to get this work done by Friday?"[GGL]

kick butts — to be impressive; ~ to be decisively good or pleasant Eg."That left foot needs to be used to kick right dems butts into gear."[DK]

out on one's butt — having been kicked out of one's residence, place of work, or position Eg."She would have to do everything at the direct discretion of the President or she'd be out on her butt."[DK]

rebutted — claim or prove that (evidence or an accusation) was false; ~ drive back or repel (a person or attack) Eg."At every turn, Biden attacked, listened, rebutted and then attacked."[DK]

rebutting — claim or prove that (evidence or an accusation) is false; ~ drive back or repel (a person or attack) Eg."You'll get plenty of practice at rebutting the counter argument."[DK]

cheek

peck on the cheek — giving a quick, light kiss Eg."John gave Cindy a perfunctory peck on the cheek and the two just stood stiffly facing the audience."[HP]

chest

puff out of the chest — make bigger; ~ you fill them with air so that they look bigger Eg."They puff out their chest as if to say, Yea! His responsibility!"[DK]

claw

claws back — the recovery of money already disbursed Eg."...then the government comes in and claws back your old age pension and taxes that amount."[CAYA]

cough

cough up — give something reluctantly, especially money or information that is due or required Eg."If we want change, we have to be the change and we have to cough up the change."[DK]

cough up some more dough — hand over, deliver cough up the money; ~ to lose possession of (a ball or puck) Eg."But if it works, what the hell; ~ I'll take it and cough up some more dough."[DK]

cry

decry — publicly denounce Eg."We could decry these developments as inappropriate for a serious debate."[DK]

dead

dead serious — one is absolutely serious Eg."No, I am dead serious."[DK]

dick

be a dick — probably arrogant Eg."Don't be a dick;
 ~ be a Weiner! Stand up for health insurance
 reform."[DK]

dick-wagging — the outrageous and rowdy
 display of alpha male masculinity in a public
 setting Eg."This isn't a dick-wagging contest,
 much as you and probably Rahm Emanuel
 would like it to be."[DK]

dick head

dick head — someone who treats people unfairly
 for little or no reason Eg."Fox's supreme
 "Village Idiot", Dick[head] Morris once smartly
 said that … "[DK]

ear

a silk sow's ear — be unable to turn something
 ugly or inferior into something attractive or of
 value Eg."Unless of course he's selling a silk
 sow's ear … "[OC]

all ears — to be waiting eagerly to hear
 about something Eg."I'm all ears - tell us what
 they had to say."[GGL]

believe my ears — used for saying that someone
 is very surprised by something that they hear
 Eg."I can't believe my ears! "[DK]

better ear — (a funny way) to refer to someone
 who wasn't paying attention or listening to
 something important Eg."He has a better ear
 for domestic politics on this issue."[WP]

close your ears — to willfully ignore or refuse to listen to something or what someone is saying Eg."If you can close your ears to the conspiracy theories about his POW time."[DK]

comforting ear — someone who is willing to listen to someone else's problems Eg."He would not have had a comforting ear if I had not reached out to him."[DK]

cut off the earmark — slash the funds set aside for particular projects Eg."And cut off the earmark spigots for Blue Dogs in the House and DINOS."[DK]

ear full — an abundant or excessive amount of something heard Eg."I guess business owners were tired of getting an ear full."[DK]

earmarks — to set funds aside for a particular project Eg."Our Governor has been a "maverick" fighting federal earmarks."[DK]

earmarks — to set funds aside for a particular project Eg."This is the one where all the earmarks got thrown into."[MSN]

earmarks — to set funds aside for a particular project Eg."he said he wouldn't sign a bill with earmarks."[MSN]

earshot — the range or distance over which one can hear or be heard Eg."pulled her aside a little, out of earshot of other volunteers…"[DK]

getting an earful — you are angrily be told what the person think Eg."Bipartisan health care negotiators are aiming to cut the costs of their bill after getting an earful from voters."[DK]

giving an earful — you angrily tell the person what you think Eg."Your teacher might give the class an earful when no one has finished yesterday's homework "[GGL]

giving an earful — telling a lengthy reprimand or angry criticism Eg."Your teacher might give the class an earful when no one has finished yesterday's homework "[NA]

got in his ear — to have one's interest or attention Eg."Looks like the folks back home have gotten in his ear! "[MSN]

has his ear — he pays great attention to what you say, and often follow your advice Eg."He has his trust and his ear."[WP]

has the ear of — your ideas are listened to and considered important by that person Eg."He has the ear of both the Senate and the White House."[DK]

have his ear — have access to and influence with someone Eg."But most of those on Obama's team who will have his ear everyday will be old friends and experienced advisers."[MSN]

rabbit ears — an acute sense of hearing or awareness of one's surroundings causing distraction or loss of focus Eg."I feel the same. Refuse to pay. Use rabbit ears in and a box."[DK]

sensitive ears — noise sensitivity Eg."Notley mentioning the words White Supremacists and that was it for her sensitive ears! "[CAAB]

ear hand

up to my ears — to be very busy, or to have more of something than you can manage Eg."I told my friend I left Indiana because I had it up to my ears."[DK]

elbow

elbowed her way in — to force one's way in Eg."She did not stumble into a boys' club. She elbowed her way in, smiling."[NWC]

picking sharp-elbowed — willing to push other people out of the way to get what one wants Eg."He moves from candidate to president-elect, picking sharp-elbowed Washington insiders for top posts."[DK]

rub elbows — associate or come into contact with another person Eg."That good fortune has meant I've gotten to rub elbows with Solis at a few private parties."[DK]

to elbow my way — to force one's way in, to, or through a crowded place, as by pushing other people with one's elbows Eg."Just going to elbow my way in here."[DK]

eye

anger in his eyes — seeing distaste with the eyes Eg."The anger and resentment in the eyes are the same between McWorse and Nixon."[HP]

before our eyes — right in front of one (used for emphasis, especially in the context of something surprising or unpleasant) Eg."It's shape shifting before our eyes."[DK]

believe my eyes and ears — being surprised at or upset by something seen or heard Eg."I remember watching that, not believing my eyes and ears."[DK]

black eye — a mark or source of dishonor or shame; ~ an area of bruised skin around the eye resulting from a blow Eg."She suspects a teacher of her son Aiden placed a complaint after he came to school with a black eye."[HP]

black eye — a mark or source of dishonor or shame; ~ an area of bruised skin around the eye resulting from a blow Eg."The paper and its employees had sustained "a huge black eye." "[HP]

blinky-eye — a brief period of time, instant; ~ blink sense Eg."What was with the blinky-eye thing McCain does? "[HP]

bulls eye — the center of the target in sports such as archery, shooting, and darts; ~ a large, round, hard peppermint-flavored candy Eg."Arlen's ad budget would be as small as the bulls eye you've painted on your back is big."[PC]

caught the eye — to get someone's attention Eg."It was in that role that Gibbs caught the eye of Jim Jordan, who hired him."[WP]

dagger-eyed (gasp) — to look at someone in a way that shows you are very angry with them Eg."Joe Wilson's outburst Wednesday night earned more than a personal rebuke from the president and a dagger-eyed gasp from the speaker of the House "[PC]

dry eye — to stop crying, wipe away tears from one's eyes Eg. "There won't be a dry eye in the room," said Valerie Jarrett, "[BC]

dry eye — to stop crying, wipe away tears from one's eyes Eg. "Not a dry eye at the ceremony.. including me!" shared Blackburn on Face book."[CAYA]

eye opening — (of an event or situation) unexpectedly enlightening Eg. "One of my eye opening experience was a next door neighbor who did not marry his wife."[NA]

eyehole — a hole to pass through or to look through, especially in a curtain or mask Eg." Binns had money, gardening gloves and a snood with eyeholes, and bags containing a jemmie bar, cash and fragrances."[TBC]

eyeing — It refers to a way that someone looks at someone they are attracted to or something that they like/desire. Eg. "The Liberals are obviously eyeing an election in the spring. "[CANP]

eye-opener — an event or situation that proves to be unexpectedly enlightening; ~ an alcoholic drink taken early in the day Eg. "His analysis of how Republicans got themselves into this mess is bound to be an eye-opener."[DK]

eye-popping — astonishingly or strikingly impressive Eg. "anticipated meeting of potential vice presidents ever, sure to be watched by millions and garner eye-popping ratings."[HP]

eyes of — in the view or opinion of, from the standpoint of Eg."Wake up to find out that you are the eyes of the world."[DK]

eyes of the world — be heard as conveying a message of hope Eg."Wake up to find out that you are the eyes of the world."[DK]

eye-to-eye — agree with each other, have the same opinion Eg."Hillary, being a scary, cold, experienced, intelligent woman, could have stood eye-to-eye with the "soccer mom" from Alaska."[DK]

fire in his eyes — having the passion, feeling and / or energy Eg."Plouffe, in particular, looked like a true diehard with fire in his eyes."[NEWSY]

give eye contact — with someone, you look at them at the same time as they look at you, so that you are both aware that you are looking at each other Eg."It's the dog's responsibility to sit and give eye contact in this situation."[DK]

glee in eyes — a brief and subtle expression in one's eye(s) indicating a hidden or secret emotion, agenda, idea, plan Eg."You could see the glee in the douche bag's eyes."[DK]

glimmer in one's eye — an expression in one's eyes that shows that one is amused or that one has a secret Eg."I would be the first in line getting a 3 months' supply...proudly...with a smile on my face and a glimmer in my eye."[DK]

in the eye — in the center or focal point of
something Eg."On McCain refusing to look
Obama in the eye "[HP]

in the eye — in the center or focal point of
something Eg."Obama has made it clear he is
willing to look our nation's adversaries in the
eye and, without fear, confront them face to
face in pursuit of our interests."[HP]

in the eye and face to face — to talk to
someone in a direct and confident way that
shows you are honest or not ashamed
Eg."Obama has made it clear he is willing to
look our nation's adversaries in the eye and,
without fear, confront them face to face in
pursuit of our interests."[HP]

in the eyes of — In the center or focal point of
something, as in they were right in the eye of
this controversy Eg."And what will destroy
Sarah in the eyes of the American people will
be if they perceive her as false … "[RSC]

in their eyes — to indicate that you are reporting
someone's opinion and that other people
might think differently Eg."Obama's refusal to
back down under pressure seems to be a sign
of weakness in right-winger's eyes."[DK]

keep an eye — watch something or someone
carefully Eg."It is from Alaska that we send
those out to make sure that an eye is being
kept on this."[NYTC]

keep the eye of — keep under careful
observation Eg."Keep the eye of centrists and
Blue Dogs on the central idea."[DK]

look in the eye — to talk to someone in an honest way that shows no doubts Eg."It was Obama who while looking us in the eye gave us some "straight talk"."[DK]

look in their eyes — to talk to someone in an honest way that shows no doubts Eg."They had this look in their eyes, totally cold, animal."[DK]

my eyes roll — usually as an expression of exasperation, annoyance, impatience, or disdain Eg."that if it makes my eyes roll the public will like it... "[DK]

opened her eyes — to see or realize the truth about something Eg."Her sojourn in the medical world as a breast cancer patient opened her eyes."[DK]

our eyes focus — be on the alert; ~ watch carefully or vigilantly for something Eg."We need to keep our eyes focused beyond the town hall meetings."[DK]

parent's eyes — from parents perspective or point of view Eg."Great analysis through the lens of your parents' eyes."[DK]

private eye — a private investigator Eg."Guergis scandal focus riles private eye."[CBC]

public eye — in a position that receives a lot of public notice and attention Eg."Many of these documents were redacted expressly to protect the identity of individuals not already in the public eye."[DK]

red-eyed — refers to a late night flight that arrives early in the morning Eg."As Woods said weeks ago, when he gave a red-eyed, televised apology to family and friends.."[MSN]

roll someone's eyes — to move eyes around in a circle because someone has said or done something stupid or strange Eg."guard as a lot of people on the left roll their eyes at any appeal to patriotism and national pride…"[DK]

rolled eyes — to turn one's eyes upward or around in a circle, usually as an expression of exasperation, annoyance, impatience, or disdain Eg."Phelps rolled his eyes and said nearly everything written about him was false."[MSN]

see eye to eye — have similar views or attitudes to something; ~ be in full agreement Eg."The two did not see eye to eye when Klein was in power."[CAAB]

see eye-to-eye — have similar views or attitudes to something; ~ be in full agreement Eg."The question is can the Coalition, which is patched together by parties that normally don't see eye-to-eye… "[DK]

snake eyes — the worst possible result; ~ a complete lack of success Eg."I had already decided that a roll of the dice on Obama was better than guaranteed snake-eyes with McCain."[DK]

snake eyes — the worst possible result; ~ a complete lack of success Eg."VP Debate: McCain's Big Gamble Comes Up Snake Eyes "[HP]

tears in his eyes — crying Eg."The then new president-elect actually had tears in his eyes when he introduced Powell."[NWC]

teary eyed — having eyes that are wet with tears Eg."I'm all teary eyed."[CAYA]

wide, sad eyes — marked by having unsophisticated or uncritical sad expression Eg."I look at him/her and say (with a straight face and wide, sad eyes)."[DK]

eye face

wide-eyed — having one's eyes wide open in amazement; ~ innocent Eg."You could have heard a pin drop. My husband, who was wide-eyed, pressed him for details."[DK]

eyeball

eyeball to eyeball — face to face with someone, especially in an aggressive way Eg."If John McCain can't go eyeball to eyeball with a fellow American in a moderated debate... "[HP]

eyeball to eyeball and face down — deal with someone in a direct way Eg."If John McCain can't go eyeball to eyeball with a fellow American in a moderated debate, how will he face down Vladimir Putin or Mahmoud Ahmadinejad "[HP]

eyeballing — look or stare at closely Eg. "Al Franken moving into a fresh phase of the struggle: eyeballing the first of 2.9 million ballots."[HP]

eyeball-to-eyeball — face to face with someone, especially in an aggressive way Eg. "In that version of the public option, it would compete eyeball-to-eyeball with the private plans."[DK]

eyebrow

furrowing eyebrows — being annoyed, unhappy, or confused Eg. "We've been furrowing our eyebrows a lot lately as we watch the McCain campaign re-write Alaska history."[DK]

raised eyebrows — to react with surprise or mild disapproval Eg. "That has raised so many eyebrows, between Obama and the pharm companies."[DK]

raised eyebrows — to react with surprise or mild disapproval Eg. "Obama raised eyebrows this month when he tapped some of Clinton's closest allies for important jobs."[MSN]

raised eyebrows — to react with surprise or mild disapproval Eg. "Karzai has raised eyebrows in Washington with recent trips to Iran, China and Pakistan."[MSN]

eyelash

parsing eyelash — flirting with or feign romantic interest in someone Eg. "I am not into parsing the eyelash of a gnat over this."[DK]

face

a face wash — of a business, to break even financially Eg."During the pileup around the Boston net, Bergeron had been trying to give Burrows a face wash."[CBC]

a false face — a caricature of human or animal features that is made of cloth, plaster Eg."The urge to save humanity is almost always a false face for the urge to rule it."[DK]

a fresh face — having a young, healthy, and innocent appearance Eg."Palin, by contrast, uses a heck of a lot of language to praise herself as a fresh face with new ideas."[NYTC]

a straight face and wide, sad eyes — a blank or serious facial expression, especially when trying not to laugh Eg."I look at him/her and say (with a straight face and wide, sad eyes)."[DK]

at face value — for the price that is printed on something; ~ as true or genuine without being questioned or doubted Eg."an anonymous White House staffer at face value? So cynical! "[DK]

bald-faced lie — showing no shame or embarrassment about doing something bad Eg."Nick Nurse calls report on Nate Bjorkgren's time in Toronto a 'bald-faced lie'."[CAYA]

call to his face — directly to him, without trying to hide anything or be kind Eg."No one ever called him a liar to his face even when he was blatantly doing it."[DK]

defacing — spoil the surface or appearance of (something), for example by drawing or writing on it Eg."Defacing other people's stuff for Obama watch: get used to it."[RSC]

egg on his face — to look foolish or be embarrassed Eg."But to whatever degree he viewed the Raptors as a non-contender, he has egg on his face."[NEWSY]

face — confront and deal with or accept a difficult or unpleasant task, fact, or situation Eg."Face the American Public "[DK]

face — confront and deal with or accept a difficult or unpleasant task, fact, or situation Eg."Face the Nation" [DK]

face — confront and deal with or accept a difficult or unpleasant task, fact, or situation Eg."You should have seen the girl's face, but it did get changed."[DK]

face — confront and deal with or accept a difficult or unpleasant task, fact, or situation Eg."then they face generic competition "[DK]

face — confront and deal with or accept a difficult or unpleasant task, fact, or situation Eg."But he could also face a rival power center within his own administration with her on his team."[HP]

face down — with the face or surface turned toward the ground Eg."How will he face down Putin or Ahmadinejad."[HP]

face it — used to say it's necessary to understand something is true and accept it Eg."Well, I think they've got it, just not the way they wanted it -- let's face it."[DK]

face it — used to say it's necessary to understand something is true and accept it Eg."Let's face it, Rahmbo (the Blue Dog cuddler) has been pretty disappointing too."[DK]

face it — used to say it's necessary to understand something is true and accept it Eg."Face it. He's chicken."[HP]

face off — take up an attitude of confrontation, especially at the start of a fight or game; ~ start or restart play with a face-off Eg."The extensive interview went over last night's Vice-Presidential face off... "[EB]

face to face — (of a situation) characterized by having those involved close together and facing each other; ~ so as to be close together and facing each other Eg."Obama has made it clear he is willing to look our nation's adversaries in the eye and, without fear, confront them face to face in pursuit of our interests."[HP]

face, faced — be positioned with the face or front toward (someone or something); ~ confront and deal with or accept a difficult or unpleasant task, fact, or situation Eg."A President Obama will face problems graver than those faced by any new president in over 60 years."[HP]

faced — confront and deal with or accept a difficult or unpleasant task, fact, or situation Eg."He faced little public opposition."[CAGLB]

faced — confront and deal with or accept a difficult or unpleasant task, fact, or situation Eg."Faced with either having to do something [which was GWB's plan] or doing nothing [because "there is no crisis"]."[DK]

faced — confront and deal with or accept a difficult or unpleasant task, fact, or situation Eg."Vote against the President, if faced with a bill without a public option."[DK]

faced — confront and deal with or accept a difficult or unpleasant task, fact, or situation Eg."so when Clinton faced a Democratic Congress on taking office..."[DMC]

faced with — to apply or attach something to the surface of something; ~ to show someone the proof of something Eg."I've seen this kind of bluster and flustered look with numerous "leaders" when faced with questions and challenge."[NA]

faceoff — take up an attitude of confrontation, especially at the start of a fight or game Eg."He is one of the league's best faceoff men."[CBC]

faceoff — take up an attitude of confrontation, especially at the start of a fight or game Eg."as they incompetently try to face off against a force of nature they have no chance of defeating."[MSN]

faces — confront and deal with or accept a difficult or unpleasant task, fact, or situation Eg."Guergis faces RCMP probe."[CBC]

faces — confront and deal with or accept a difficult or unpleasant task, fact, or situation Eg."The New York Times today reports that Romney's faces a "daunting path" in a campaign that is "tilting against him."[DK]

faces — confront and deal with or accept a
difficult or unpleasant task, fact, or situation
Eg."Health plans recognize the significant
hardship that a family faces."[HP]

faces — confront and deal with or accept a
difficult or unpleasant task, fact, or situation
Eg."The nomination slipped out of her reach
last spring she spoke of the threats this
country faces."[HP]

faces — confront and deal with or accept a difficult
or unpleasant task, fact, or situation
Eg."America faces great challenges in the
months and years ahead."[MSN]

face-saving — the preserving of one's reputation,
credibility, or dignity Eg."which was in many
ways tangential to the point we were arguing
about anyway, and thus provided a graceful
"face-saving" way out if needed."[DK]

face wash — of a business, to break even
financially Eg."after a face wash competition
between the two at the end of the first period
during the Canucks... "[CBC]

facing — positioned with the front toward a
certain direction; ~ opposite Eg."news reports
and economic charts revealing the grim facts
facing most Americans... "[DK]

facing — positioned with the front toward a
certain direction; ~ opposite Eg."turning to
McCain, not to Obama, for advice when facing
"the toughest decision of your life "[DMC]

facing — positioned with the front toward a
certain direction; ~ opposite Eg."Facing a post
convention fall in the polls, John McCain once

again reshaped the dimensions of the
race..."[DMC]

facing — positioned with the front toward a
certain direction; ~ opposite Eg."The Dems
agreed to the price tag while Bush agreed to
special aid to families facing
foreclosure."[DMC]

facing — positioned with the front toward a
certain direction; ~ opposite Eg."He took time
to speak respectfully about McCain while
having no trouble facing him, regardless of
the issue."[HP]

facing — positioned with the front toward a
certain direction; ~ opposite Eg."John gave
Cindy a perfunctory peck on the cheek and
the two just stood stiffly facing the
audience."[HP]

flew in the face — to completely oppose what
seems sensible or normal Eg."but because it
flew in the face of the alleged caution "[HP]

gut wrenching — extremely unpleasant or
upsetting Eg."and an absolutely gut
wrenching ending "[DK]

in our faces — attitude seems determined to
behave in a way that is unusual or shocking,
and does not care what people think of them
Eg."Progressives now will continue to demand
that level of moral high ground which was so
oft flouted in our faces."[DK]

in the face of — when confronted with Eg."To
show what true progressives do in the face of
racism."[DK]

in the face of — when confronted with Eg. "If she thinks she can sway people by repeating "it's dangerous" in the face of overwhelming evidence to the contrary." [DK]

in the face of — when confronted with Eg. "the need for new revenue in the face of a soaring budget deficit." [DK]

in the face of — when confronted with Eg. "may prove insurmountable this year in the face of mounting budget deficits " [DK]

in your face — directly at or against one; ~ as one approaches Eg. "He would get in your face, not in a very heated way, but he would question your stories." [WP]

laughable on its face — from only what is known at first Eg. "to use a word that surprisingly was not used during last night's debate, literally laughable on its face " [DK]

lie to his face — to tell a lie directly to someone without trying to hide it Eg. "They can lie to his face and he still wants to play patty cake." [DK]

long faces — an unhappy or disappointed expression Eg. "You do not see much long faces." [NA]

might face — confront and deal with or accept a difficult or unpleasant task, fact, or situation Eg. "Leno might face resistance from O'Brien's fans." [HP]

new face — someone who is new in a particular public role Eg. "Republicans are desperate for, looking for the new face of politics." [PC]

on a face-off — take up an attitude of confrontation, especially at the start of a fight or game Eg."After all, this is the guy that the Republicans want to send on a face-off with Putin...right? "[DK]

on its face — direct and forceful, in a way that might shock or offend some people Eg."This is silly on its face."[DK]

on the face — without knowing all of the relevant facts; ~ at first glance Eg."Mud may sound like it doesn't belong on the face, but any skin guru will tell you to think again! "[TBC]

on their faces — aggressively unavoidable; ~ thrust upon one's attention Eg."The two just stood stiffly facing the audience with death-skull grins on their faces."[HP]

on their faces — aggressively unavoidable; ~ thrust upon one's attention Eg."The many pundits who now have egg on their faces for their early hailing of Palin and/or predictions of how strongly she would help the ticket."[HP]

public face — a spokesperson, a person that represents an organization to the public Eg."The 37-year-old Alabama native is about to become the public face of the Obama administration."[WP]

punched in the face — it is more like an expression, usually meaning something like a 'shock' Eg."He could deliver a harsh message, but do it with a little sense of humor, so you'd feel punched in the stomach but not in the face."[WP]

red faced — (of a person) having a red face, especially as a result of exertion, embarrassment, or shame Eg."He might have one of those red-faced, finger-pointing moments about Obama."[HP]

red-faced, finger-pointing — blushing or flushed with embarrassment, anger, resentment, or the like Eg."He might have one of those red-faced, finger-pointing moments about Obama."[HP]

save face — retain respect; ~ avoid humiliation Eg."Are these real changes or are they just cosmetic changes and an effort to save face?"[DK]

save face — retain respect; ~ avoid humiliation Eg."W. on Iraq that the only way to beat an insurgency and save face is to stick it out "[NYTC]

shame faced — feeling or expressing shame or embarrassment Eg."But as the shamefaced reporter told me, even someone reading the 2 stories together."[CAAB]

should face — have to deal with Eg."others should face a diagnosis of life threatening illness or injury "[DK]

slap in the face — an unexpected rejection or affront Eg."opposition to the 2008 auto industry bailout and called it a slap in the face of every Michigan worker."[REU]

slapped in the face — a surprising act that offends or insults someone Eg."when they get slapped in the face with obvious stupid masquerading "[DK]

smack in the face — something that will humiliate someone, often when it is considered deserved; ~ an insult Eg."Energy experts smack Albertans in the face with call to get ready for transition to a new energy world."[CAGLB]

smile on my face glimmer in my eye — to please someone or make someone happy Eg."I would be the first in line getting a 3 months supply...proudly...with a smile on my face and a glimmer in my eye "[DK]

smile on my face — to please someone or make someone happy Eg."I would be the first in line getting a 3 months supply...proudly...with a smile on my face and a glimmer in my eye "[DK]

smiling face — often expresses genuine happiness and warm, positive feelings Eg."that smiling face, those novel phrases, that informal style "[DK]

spit in his face — to show extreme contempt or scorn for Eg."his constant sucking up to the right (which spit in his face, BTW) "[DK]

start facing — to begin a competition or contest Eg."he'd have to start facing himself, and the corruptness of his own pov would crumble "[DK]

straight face — an emotionless facial expression, especially in a humorous situation that could easily cause one to laugh Eg."I look at him/her and say (with a straight face and wide, sad eyes) "[DK]

straight face — an emotionless facial expression, especially in a humorous situation that could easily cause one to laugh Eg."I mean, how do these guys stand there with a straight face and moan about public dollars."[DK]

straight face (test) — a test of whether something is legitimate or serious based on whether a given statement or legal argument can be made sincerely, without any compulsion to laugh Eg."like those for mortgage interest and the like doesn't pass the straight face test. It's comical."[DK]

to face — confront and deal with or accept a difficult or unpleasant task, fact, or situation Eg."must have lies ghost written for you and you don't have to face anyone that could refute them."[DK]

to some one's face — to say something (unpleasant) directly to someone Eg."Will no one confront this bizarre babe, right to her face? "[TBC]

feet

both feet back — well or successful again after being ill or having problems Eg."The Boston Bruins have both feet back in this Stanley Cup Final."[CBC]

cold feet — a loss or lack of courage or confidence; ~ an onset of uncertainty or fear Eg."Jaffer to testify in Guergis affair, despite cold feet at NDP "[CAYA]

cold feet — a loss or lack of courage or confidence; ~ an onset of uncertainty or fear Eg."Amendment didn't apply to this case, but they got cold feet when the Amendment was enforced in two other actions by the Pentagon."[DK]

feet on the ground — you approve of the fact that they have a sensible and practical attitude towards life, and do not have unrealistic ideas Eg."And that means money and feet on the ground lost and primary challengers put forth."[DK]

feet to the fire — pressure someone to consent to or undertake something Eg."We will hold the administration & Congressional Dems who made promises to the middle class' feet to the fire."[DK]

hold feet to fire — pressure someone to consent to or undertake something Eg."We will hold his feet to the fire."[CAGLB]

off their feet — so as to be no longer standing Eg."But Barack Obama is just one of the latest to knock a few off their feet "[ABC]

off their feet — so as to be no longer standing Eg."what it was that swept America off their feet when they first met Sarah "[RSC]

on feet — in a healthy or stable condition, usually after a period of illness or misfortune Eg."It is better to die on your feet than to live on your knees."[DK]

on feet than on knees — you would rather keep your dignity and suffer, even to the 'end! ', rather than ask for help, or beg for charity

Eg."It is better to die on your feet than to live on your knees."[DK]

quick on his feet — sharp-witted Eg."I was surprised (more during the extra session than what aired) by how quick on his feet Stewart was to shoot down some of her facts "[DK]

stomp their feet — to put a foot down on the ground hard and quickly, making a loud noise, often to show anger Eg."They decided to play politics and stomp their feet like little children."[DK]

their feet — standing; ~ well enough after an illness or injury to walk around Eg."A lot of political speakers bring people to their feet."[ABC]

think on his feet — react to events decisively, effectively, and without prior thought or planning Eg."He has demonstrated time and again he can think on his feet."[MYDD]

finger

finger — to have an interest in or be involved in everything Eg."We really need to get a finger on what's going on here."[DK]

finger in your eye — deliberately provoking someone Eg."And in a "here's a finger in your eye buddy" move, he also proposed eliminating the traditional government."[DK]

finger pointing — actions or words that bring attention to a particular person or issue Eg."He might have one of those red-faced, finger-pointing moments about Obama."[HP]

fingered — to identify (someone) as responsible for some crime or wrongdoing Eg."Biting flies growing on pig feces in overflowing unsanitary waste ponds have been fingered as the vector of interspecies viral mixing."[DK]

finger-pointing — actions or words that bring attention to a particular person or issue Eg."obviously not ready for the finger-pointing and whispers that would come her way "[MSN]

fingerprints — an impression or mark made (on a surface) by a person Eg."You can see the fingerprints in the deals that they made."[DK]

fingers on their backbones — to work extremely hard, especially for a long time Eg."Democratic colleagues who couldn't quite put their fingers on their backbones to deny him a committee chairmanship "[MN]

give finger — to raise the middle finger (a rude gesture of anger or displeasure) at one; ~ to treat one poorly or display contempt for one Eg."He gave me finger."[NA]

lift a finger for us — to make an effort to do something —usually used in negative statements Eg."There's just not a lot of expectation they are going to lift a finger for us."[PC]

point a finger — to accuse or blame (someone) Eg."But Newsweek's epic account of Obama's campaign this week points a finger at Clinton's top strategist."[CBS]

point fingers — to indicate that one is guilty of (doing) something; ~ to blame or accuse one of (doing) something Eg."He isn't the only one to blame for the banks failing and standing around pointing fingers hardly helps."[DK]

point her finger — she indicates that one is guilty of (doing) something; ~ to blame or accuse one of (doing) something Eg."I hated how she kept pointing her finger at John Stewart."[DK]

put a finger on — to discover the exact reason why a situation is the way it is, especially when something is wrong Eg."She probably couldn't put a finger on what bothered her about McCain."[DK]

put their fingers on — to discover the exact reason why a situation is the way it is, especially when something is wrong Eg."Democratic colleagues who couldn't quite put their fingers on their backbones to deny him a committee chairmanship."[MN]

showed his finger to — to discover the exact reason why a situation is the way it is, especially when something is wrong Eg."Bergeron took off his glove and showed his finger to referees."[CBC]

tip of fingers — (especially of information) readily available; ~ accessible Eg."Fortunately we don't have to imagine it, because we already have that potential at the tip of our voting fingers."[HP]

wag of the finger — you shake it repeatedly and quickly from side to side, usually because you are annoyed with someone Eg."has given

Canadians a strict wag of the finger for denying the American squad ice time at the Olympic oval in Richmond, B.C."[CBC]

fist

clenched fist — to show extreme anger or resentment Eg."President Obama held out his open hand as a gesture of his willing to be bipartisan and the Republicans responded with a clenched fist."[DK]

foot

a foot fault — an infraction of the service rules Eg."She looked straight to the camera. I didn't see a foot fault in the whole thing."[HB]

a foot-in-the-door — to make the first step toward a goal by gaining entry into an organization Eg."It could very well end up being a foot-in-the-door moment for us."[DK]

afoot — happening, or being planned or prepared Eg."and the game is afoot "[DK]

dead foot — very tired but still standing, working Eg."As an "old school" pilot I was always taught to go "dead foot, dead engine" when I was learning."[CAYA]

dead foot — very tired but still standing, working Eg."Satan....I, too, was taught the "dead foot" protocol in my multi training."[CAYA]

flat-footed — clumsy, awkward, or uninspired; ~ slow to react; ~ unprepared Eg."And as a result we were kind of caught flat-footed on some of these tapes."[CAYA]

flat-footed — clumsy, awkward, or uninspired; ~ slow to react; ~ unprepared Eg."But Lucic, lacking the skills of an experienced blue-liner, was flat-footed and couldn't do much."[CBC]

flat-footed — clumsy, awkward, or uninspired; ~ slow to react; ~ unprepared Eg."bully caught flat-footed in her own bullshit "[DK]

followed footsteps — to do the same things that another person has done before Eg."She followed in her dad's footsteps."[STBC]

foot dragging — to procrastinate or do something very slowly (or not complete it) because you don't want to do it Eg."Maybe it's really in the works and a lot of the foot dragging is just to get the public ready for it."[DK]

foot dragging — to procrastinate or do something very slowly (or not complete it) because you don't want to do it Eg."I really believe in consequences for the oversized egos and foot dragging."[DK]

foot dragging — to procrastinate or do something very slowly (or not complete it) because you don't want to do it Eg."We're so tired of them and their purposeful foot-dragging...enough already."[DK]

foot in the mouth — say something foolish, embarrassing, or tactless Eg."He finds out another tidbit from the amazing foot in mouth machine that is Sarah Palin."[DK]

foot on banana peel — to be at risk of sudden change, unstable Eg."It was a simple step forward, nothing more, but at least his foot didn't land on a banana peel."[MSN]

footage — a length of film made for movies or television Eg."perhaps the most embarrassing footage ever..."[DK]

footage — a length of film made for movies or television Eg."So, that un-aired footage that CBS has of Couric interviewing Caribou Barbie."[DK]

footage — a length of film made for movies or television Eg."in his biography and also in interview footage I've seen of him "[DK]

footage — a length of film made for movies or television Eg."Footage was played during the trial, although members of the gallery could only hear the audio."[NEWSY]

footage — a length of film made for movies or television Eg."But there is footage of him as a 33-year-old elected politician."[TWT]

foothold — to obtain an initial, stable position from which one can progress in a particular industry or area Eg."When you have Sean Hannity and The Daily Kos on the same side you know your political foothold is about as solid as quicksand."[SYPC]

footing — to slip, stumble, and/or fall during an activity Eg."How Woods' would regain his footing after a stunning fall from grace five months ago has been answered."[MSN]

footnote — that you are adding some information that is related to what has just been mentioned Eg."SNC Lavalin will become a footnote for the federal election."[CBC]

footnote — that you are adding some information that is related to what has just been mentioned Eg."upon starting his election bid may seem like a mildly relevant footnote in an otherwise sad family drama."[HP]

in the foot — foolishly harm one's own cause Eg."Talk about shooting yourselves in the foot in the name of ideological purity."[DK]

keep a foot — to maintain one's balance; ~ to avoid falling or tripping Eg."A country that has given a lot of us reasons to wonder if there is much to be proud of, as many attempt to keep a foot grinding us into the dust."[DK]

left foot — be clumsy Eg."That left foot needs to be used to kick right dems butts into gear."[DK]

left foot — be clumsy Eg."If we are serious about change, someone needs to inform Rahm that he has a left foot."[DK]

on the right foot — be in a positive or favorable position Eg."And she got her ticket off on the right foot for October - making the tax issue stick."[DMC]

one foot outside — someone who is half in and half out Eg."Obama will come to Washington, but will keep one foot outside the Beltway."[DMC]

put foot down — to act firmly / to tell someone strongly that they must do something or that they must stop doing something Eg."Mr. Harper has earned some brownie points from me for putting his foot down on this scandalous issue."[CBC]

set foot — enter it or reach it Eg."Someone please fix New Orelans I will never set foot in Las Vegas and yes I know I am screaming."[DK]

set foot — enter it or reach it Eg."It's a part of the country she's mostly avoided since 2008, conspicuously not setting foot in early... "[PC]

shoot in the foot — foolishly harm one's own cause Eg."I just love watching the repugnant ones shoot themselves in the foot "[MSN]

shooting ones own foot — foolishly harm one's own cause Eg."These guys are shooting themselves in the foot over and over on this one."[DK]

shooting yourself in the foot — foolishly harm one's own cause Eg."They are untouchable but this has to be the most stunning example of hubris and shooting yourself in the foot."[DK]

shoots in the foot — foolishly harm one's own cause Eg."The US government once again shoots itself in the foot and creates another enemy."[DK]

underfoot — under one's feet; ~ on the ground; ~ constantly present and in one's way Eg."The giants have discovered that the individuals underfoot have created grappling hooks and lines."[DK]

foot-mouth

put foot on the mouth — say something foolish, embarrassing, or tactless Eg."though Clinton also did manage to put her own foot in her mouth a few times early on "[NWC]

gullets

gullets — for something to bother one after it has happened Eg."to provide us the facts while instead pouring propaganda down our gullets "[DK]

gut

a gut sense — a personal, intuitive feeling an instinctive feeling, without any logical rationale Eg."A gut sense of Americanism is a hard thing for someone like Barack Obama."[PC]

go on gut instinct — go on your immediate understanding of something Eg."He tends to shoot from the hip and go on gut instinct."[MYDD]

gut — instinct Eg."Do you think its just coincidence that we collapsed GWB's plan to gut Social Security? "[DK]

gut feeling — a personal, intuitive instinctive feeling, without any logical rationale Eg."Your gut feeling tells you he's being genuine and real."[MSN]

gut instincts — your immediate understanding of something Eg."Rahm's gut instincts knew that taking KSM to New York for civilian trials was going to be a misstep."[WP]

gutless — lacking courage or determination Eg."I agree that Harry Reid is a spineless, gutless idiot."[DK]

guts — a feeling or reaction based on an instinctive emotional response rather than considered thought Eg."One Congressman with guts stood up to them: Congressman Alan Grayson."[DK]

guts — a feeling or reaction based on an instinctive emotional response rather than considered thought Eg."at least O'Reilly has the guts to yell at children and cut off mics..."[DK]

guts — a feeling or reaction based on an instinctive emotional response rather than considered thought Eg."Idiots in Washington don't have the guts to admit what everybody knows."[DK]

guts — a feeling or reaction based on an instinctive emotional response rather than considered thought Eg."Glad people like this vet have the guts to stand up to these stupid little punks."[DMUK]

gutted — cause (someone) to feel extremely upset or disappointed Eg."to protect public-sector pension plans from being gutted by future governments "[CAAB]

gutted — cause (someone) to feel extremely upset or disappointed Eg."We will see our major social programs gutted but almost no investment outside oil and gas."[NYB]

have the guts — to have courage or boldness Eg."All he has to do is have the guts to do what he didn't have the courage to do in the debate: Play the hand."[DMC]

punched in the gut — something that affects you strongly in an emotional sense Eg."But we, on the left, despite being punched in the gut repeatedly every time… "[DK]

takes guts — requires courage in the face of danger or great risk Eg."That takes guts to put your own feelings aside and focus on what really mattered that day."[CAYA]

to gut — cause (someone) to feel extremely upset or disappointed Eg."While Jason Kenney plans to gut our current services… "[CAAB]

hair

a box of hair — used to insult someone's intelligence level and comprehension of common sense Eg."college educated, dumber than a box of hair..."[DK]

a hair late — by an extremely short or slim margin Eg."perhaps it was a hair late -- open-ice hit."[CBC]

a hair's-breadth — a very small amount or margin Eg."With polls showing Santorum within a hair's-breadth of achieving an upset win in Romney's home state, the stakes could not be higher on Tuesday."[REU]

by a hair — very narrowly Eg."It's tied - actually Barack winning by a hair "[DK]

crosshairs — in a position where one might receive sever criticism Eg."Perry repeatedly found himself in the crosshairs, as the field of candidates took turns attacking his positions."[CNN]

crosshairs — in a position where one might receive sever criticism Eg."Now Paterson is in Obama's cross hairs."[NYDC]

hair on fire — impassioned, wild, crazy, rage-filled, frantic Eg."Run around! Your hair is on fire! It's not my fault, it's their fault."[DK]

hair on fire — impassioned, wild, crazy, rage-filled, frantic Eg."like stupid Dkos bloggers lighting their hair on fire "[DK]

hair trigger — a trigger of a firearm set for release at the slightest pressure; ~ liable to change suddenly and violently Eg."What is going to happen when we get that same president, but with a hair trigger temper? "[DK]

hairdo — the way in which a person's hair is styled Eg."This customer seems to have two separate hairdos, neither cooperating with the other."[TBC]

hairdresser — a person who cuts and styles hair as an occupation Eg."another customer too lazy to book a hairdresser appointment "[TBC]

hairs on neck stand up — to scare or horrify someone Eg."when the hairs on Christian necks stand up—they rush to repeat what has become their mantra "[FC]

knockout hair — for Men is a sports-themed, full-service salon providing Precision haircut Eg."There was a handsome, rich Prince with knockout hair, "[HP]

split hairs — make small and unnecessary distinctions Eg."Yes, let's split hairs over the additive that make smoking tolerable."[DK]

hand

a backhanded — indirect; ~ ambiguous or insincere Eg."That sounds like a backhanded compliment."[HP]

a handful — a person who is very difficult to deal with or control Eg."It's foolish to think that a handful of people canceling their policies will really have the effect you want."[DK]

a handful of — a small quantity or number Eg."He or she will have seniority over a handful of other Democrats who will take the oath of office in January."[HP]

a steady hand on — a situation in which someone is keeping good control of a situation Eg."Senator Obama has been doing what he does best: keeping a steady hand on the wheel."[DK]

ahead — further forward in space or time; ~ in the line of one's forward motion or in advance; ~ in the near future Eg."Is this lady just ahead of the trend, unlike us? "[TBC]

all hands in a deck — of, relating to, or being a situation in which every available person is needed or called to assist Eg. "We need all hands on deck. We need you." [DK]

all over my hands — to be to blamed for something; ~ have responsibility for something Eg. "There's blood all over my hands in this, MacTavish said." [CAYEG]

any hands — in any (or no) way or direction; ~ on any account; ~ on no account Eg. "I'm trying to get the song into any ears and hands that can help further real health care reform for Americans." [DK]

at hand — nearby; ~ readily accessible when needed; ~ close in time; ~ about to happen Eg. "Focus on the task at hand." [HP]

at the left hand — on or toward the left side of a person or thing Eg. "Then he will say to those at his left hand, ... " [DK]

at the right hand — on or toward the right side of a person or thing Eg. "Then the King will say to those at his right hand, ... " [DK]

beforehand — before an action or event; ~ in advance Eg. "I kind of doubt this was not thought of beforehand but who cares? beautiful regardless." [CAYA]

beforehand — before an action or event; ~ in advance Eg. "There was so much talk beforehand about how Biden couldn't appear to condescend to Palin." [DK]

beforehand — before an action or event; ~ in advance Eg. "It's not germane what the discussion was beforehand." [WP]

brand new hands — new comer, novice
Eg."anybody could jump into - whether they are old hands at it - or brand new to the fight "[DK]

checkbook in hand — a book of checks with your name printed on them that is given to Eg."McCain's choice of Palin sent her running to the Obama campaign with checkbook in hand."[DK]

clapping a big hand — to applaud one extensively Eg."John, wait up," called Sen. John Kerry, D-Mass., clapping a big hand on John McCain's shoulder."[HP]

come in handy — turn out to be useful Eg."All of it will come in handy round about Sep/Oct of next year."[DK]

empty handed — having failed to obtain or achieve what one wanted Eg."Politically disastrous for Obama and his party to emerge empty handed from this year's heated battle."[DK]

first hand — coming from the original source or personal experience; ~ gained or learned directly Eg."They knew the pain and knew first hand what the Great Depression felt."[DK]

get a handle — to understand and be able to deal with (something) Eg."As a people we need to spend a lot of time and effort to get a handle on this system."[DK]

get a handle — to understand and be able to deal with (something) Eg."Is there anything on the Dems' roster that could get a decent handle before it gets to the media stage? "[DK]

give (one) a big hand — to applaud one extensively, often as a show of approval or appreciation Eg."Let's give our special guest a big hand! "[GGL]

had a hand — to be involved in (something) Eg."I can only imagine that my 18,000+$ PPO plan probably had a hand in affecting the attitudes of these professionals."[DK]

ham-handed — clumsy or bungling; ~ ham-fisted Eg."for O'Brien, widely seen as victimized by Leno and by NBC's ham-handed shake up "[HP]

hand — pick (something) up and give it to (someone) Eg."beginning with new legislation to strengthen the United States' hand against terrorists in Afghanistan "[BC]

hand and glove — in extremely close relationship or agreement working hand in glove with the police Eg."It was rumored at the time that some of the gangs were working hand in glove with the police."[GGL]

hand him — to pass or give something to someone directly Eg."The only other option was to hand him a participation ribbon."[DK]

hand in — to submit or give something to someone Eg."that he is free to hand in his resignation at any time between now and January 20th "[OC]

hand out — give a share of something or one of a set of things to each of a number of people; ~ distribute; ~ impose or inflict a penalty or misfortune on someone Eg."Too bad they didn't hand out overly ripe (but not rotten) tomatoes to the audience."[DK]

hand out — give a share of something or one of a set of things to each of a number of people; ~ distribute; ~ impose or inflict a penalty or misfortune on someone Eg."on Monday to hand out $221,000 in federal stimulus money and received high praise "[NYTC]

hand outs and hand them outs — give a share of something or one of a set of things to each of a number of people; ~ distribute; ~ impose or inflict a penalty or misfortune on someone Eg."Download these great flyers and handouts, print them and hand them out."[DK]

hand over — pass responsibility to someone else; ~give someone or something, or the responsibility for someone or something, to someone else Eg."I'll call her premier till the day she has to hand over power to Mr. Unmentionable."[CBC]

hand them out — to distribute something freely; ~ disseminate something Eg."Download these great flyers and handouts, print them and hand them out."[DK]

handbills — to give (something) to someone by hand Eg."Download these handbills and signs, print them, and hold them up at meetings and protests."[DK]

handcuffed — put handcuffs on (someone) Eg."Mr. Blagojevich was handcuffed by the agent, who was wearing a wire "[HP]

handcuffs — prohibit from belonging to the group; ~ to report, rat out to the police Eg."If this woman refuses to reform, it may be time for handcuffs."[TBC]

handed — doing or about to do something illegal or wrong or something that has a negative connotation Eg."It's true MacTavish handed Eakins a weak roster."[CAYEG]

handed — doing or about to do something illegal or wrong or something that has a negative connotation Eg."He's not just a press flunky who gets handed a piece of paper with talking points."[WP]

handed out — to give without charge; ~ to give freely; ~ administer handed out a severe punishment Eg."Checks like this are being handed out nationwide because of Arlen Specter's vote, a courageous vote, "[NYTC]

handicap — a circumstance that makes progress or success difficult; ~ act as an impediment to Eg."He has the handicap of youth and relative inexperience."[DK]

handicapped — having a condition that markedly restricts one's ability to function Eg."He seems to be posing as a handicapped shopper."[TBC]

handily — in a dexterous manner; ~ easily defeated the other candidate handily; ~ conveniently nearby Eg."While the Warriors have won each of the last two games handily, they still have a lot of work to do."[MSN]

handing — pick (something) up and give it to (someone) Eg."Summit Series for two-handing Valeri Kharlamov's ankle and taking him out of the series."[CBC]

handing out — to distribute something freely; ~ to administer or mete something Eg."We setup a recurring $20 a month or something, times all the progressives and start handing out the carrots and sticks."[DK]

handle — manage (a situation or problem); ~ the part by which a thing is held, carried, or controlled; ~ (nick) name Eg."but Beck can't even handle having an opposing viewpoint on his own show."[DK]

handle — manage (a situation or problem); ~ the part by which a thing is held, carried, or controlled; ~ (nick) name Eg."we need a President that can handle more than one crisis at a time."[HP]

handle — manage (a situation or problem); ~ the part by which a thing is held, carried, or controlled; ~ (nick) name Eg."President Palin would be desperately trying to comprehend and handle business."[HP]

handle — manage (a situation or problem); ~ the part by which a thing is held, carried, or controlled; ~ (nick) name Eg."Tonight was an illustration of how Obama and McCain handle adversaries."[HP]

handle — manage (a situation or problem); ~ the part by which a thing is held, carried, or controlled; ~ (nick) name Eg."The new president said, and he needed someone of her stature to handle foreign policy."[NWC]

handle — manage (a situation or problem); ~ the part by which a thing is held, carried, or controlled; ~ (nick) name Eg."source involved with the administration's deliberations over how to handle Paterson "[NYDC]

handle — manage (a situation or problem); ~ the part by which a thing is held, carried, or controlled; ~ (nick) name Eg."He's the last person Barack talks to when he's thinking about how to handle reporters' questions."[WP]

handle — manage (a situation or problem); ~ the part by which a thing is held, carried, or controlled; ~ (nick) name Eg."There were a couple of times that I flew off the handle."[WP]

handled — a way of dealing with something; ~ a grasp of a problem Eg."It needs to ask the tough questions and votes being handled in the senate and house."[DK]

handled — a way of dealing with something; ~ a grasp of a problem Eg."How badly the Obama administration has handled the messaging on this issue."[DK]

handled — a way of dealing with something; ~ a grasp of a problem Eg."Obama handled everything perfectly, ran his campaign with the dignity."[DK]

handled — a way of dealing with something; ~ a grasp of a problem Eg."a relative newcomer who handled communications, research and policy "[DK]

handled — a way of dealing with something; ~ a grasp of a problem Eg."She even handled Biden very well on his turf, foreign policy - meeting him head-to-head on every issue, and winning."[DMC]

handled — a way of dealing with something; ~ a grasp of a problem Eg."Woods handled everyone but the last one with relative ease."[MSN]

handled well — managed or administered efficiently Eg."But this has not been handled well from a public relations and marketing standpoint."[DK]

handler — a person who handles or deals with certain articles or commodities; ~ a person who trains or has charge of an animal Eg."Our training philosophy asks that the handler refrain from telling the dog what to do."[DK]

handler — a person who handles or deals with certain articles or commodities; ~ a person who trains or has charge of an animal Eg."Our training philosophy asks that the handler refrain from telling the dog."[DK]

handlers — someone who advises someone important Eg."We'll see if McCain's handlers will allow her to continue to hold that position tomorrow."[DK]

handles — manage (a situation or problem) Eg."Boston assistant Doug Houda (who handles the defence)… "[CBC]

handouts — something given free to a needy person or organization Eg."Download these great flyers and handouts, print them and hand them out."[DK]

handover — an act or instance of handing something over Eg."That they said that the refusal to hand over money was akin to a terrorist act."[DK]

hand-over-hand — by passing the hands alternately one before or above another Eg."Stupidity takes you in an endless hand-over-hand race."[DK]

hand-picked — select carefully with a particular purpose in mind Eg."O'Toole says a hand-picked Trudeau appointee in the top job is an unfair advantage — a conflict of interest."[CANP]

hands — pick (something) up and give it to (someone) Eg."Jason Kenney hands a challenge to Albertans."[CBC]

hands dirty — you become involved in something where the realities might compromise your principles Eg."get your hands dirty "[NA]

hands full — you are very busy because of it Eg."He had his hands full with the collapsing economy."[NWC]

hands get dirt — to get involved with all aspects of your job, including routine, practical, or more junior work Eg."The game is who wins, not whose hands get the least dirt on them."[DK]

hands off — used as a warning not to touch or interfere with something Eg."Federal government keep its hands off my medicare has only further discredited the opposition."[DK]

hands off — used as a warning not to touch or interfere with something Eg."The other school preaches, "Let Palin be Palin," a hands-off approach."[HP]

hands off — used as a warning not to touch or interfere with something Eg."He was the architect of the hands off approach to Congress with respect to HCR."[DK]

handsome — (of a man) good-looking; ~ (of a number, sum of money, or margin) substantial Eg."Handsome, charismatic candidate against a man who's neither? Well, you get the point:..."[DMC]

handsome — (of a man) good-looking; ~ (of a number, sum of money, or margin) substantial Eg."There was a handsome, rich Prince with knockout hair."[HP]

handy — convenient to handle or use; ~ useful; ~ close at hand Eg."With that in mind, I have compiled a handy resource for your perusal."[DK]

have handles — to understand and be able to deal with (something) Eg."It would be better to work on upcoming proposals and make sure they have handles that make sense."[DK]

have to hand it — they have been very successful or skilful Eg."You have to hand it to the governor: there's something to be said for brazen self-destruction."[HP]

heavy-handed — dealing with people or problems in a severe or harsh way Eg."New York Democrats were stunned by the Obama administration's heavy-handedness."[NYNC]

his hands — in one's responsibility, charge, or care Eg."I had a philosophy teacher cup his hands to have us argue about whether there was a pink elephant cupped in his hands."[DK]

in his hands — under one's control or influence Eg."I had a philosophy teacher cup his hands to have us argue about whether there was a pink elephant cupped in his hands."[DK]

in the hands of — (also in someone's hands) controlled or owned by someone Eg."The president put both the conceptual framing and the messaging for his health care plan in the hands of policy wonks."[DK]

in the hands of — (also in someone's hands) controlled or owned by someone Eg."Now Health care is all in the hands of idiots like Rahm and Reid and Bluedogs."[DK]

into his own hands — to take control of something Eg."The sight of a woman being struck was simply too much for a diner at a

Waffle House who decided to take matters into his own hands."[DMUK]

invisible hand — an unseen force or mechanism that guides individuals to unwittingly benefit society Eg."The Invisible Hand" is dependent on all players having relevant and pertinent information."[DK]

keep her hand — to remain involved in something Eg."Notice that when he first told her to show him, she kept her hand in the open section of the binder and kept talking."[DK]

lead hand — safe and timely; ~ responsible for overseeing a group of workers assigned to them Eg."Craig MacTavish, lead hand in the bucket of blood operation that is Oilers senior management."[CAYEG]

life in their hands — to do something that is very dangerous Eg."Wellpoint executives live like kings who have the lives of patients in their hands."[DK]

no hands — when someone has no street fighting skills at all Eg."This is a case of we get the stove is hot... no hands please."[DK]

offhand — ungraciously or offensively nonchalant or cool in manner; ~ without previous thought or consideration Eg."I do know off hand they have a much lower opinion of republican's than they do democrats."[DK]

off-hand — ungraciously or offensively nonchalant or cool in manner; ~ without previous thought or consideration Eg."The burns are too soon, too deep and too "off-hand"."[DK]

old hands — a person with a lot of experience in something Eg."anybody could jump into - whether they are old hands at it - or brand new to the fight "[DK]

old hands and brand new hands — persons with lots of experience in something and new comers, novices Eg."anybody could jump into - whether they are old hands at it - or brand new to the fight "[DK]

on our hands — Imposed upon one, especially as one's responsibility to confront or manage Eg."But that's what neighbors do. We have a helluva of a mess on our hands."[DK]

on the one hand — used to introduce a point of view, fact, or situation, followed by another that typically contrasts with it Eg."On the one hand, I faced the prospect of losing my day-to-day contact with the kids."[GGL]

on the other hand — used to introduce a contrasting point of view, fact, or situation Eg."On the other hand, if you have a reputation of... "[DK]

on the other hand — used to introduce a contrasting point of view, fact, or situation Eg."Kenney on the other hand, well...if you're elected by these people, you're beholden to these people."[STSB]

one hand — from one particular point of view Eg."One hand doesn't know what the other hand is doing."[DK]

one hand … other hand — from one particular point of view - highlighting a second, conflicting point of view Eg."One hand doesn't know what the other hand is doing."[DK]

one on hand — from one particular point of view Eg."One on hand I'm all for term limits - I think."[DK]

open hand — giving freely; ~ generous Eg."President Obama held out his open hand as a gesture of his willing to be bipartisan."[DK]

other hand — from a different, conflicting, or contradictory point of view Eg."One hand doesn't know what the other hand is doing."[DK]

own hands — committed by oneself or as a direct result of one's actions Eg."This woman took things into her own hands, literally. "[TBC]

play the hand — to accept, deal with, and make the most of one's current situation or circumstances Eg."All he has to do is have the guts to do what he didn't have the courage to do in the debate: Play the hand."[DMC]

press on hand — gently as a way of expressing friendship Eg."There was press on hand, but i don't know yet if anything was published."[DK]

put their hands — to undertake or apply oneself to (doing) something Eg."But the American public still doesn't get that they can't put their hands there."[DK]

shorthand — a short and simple way of
expressing or referring to something Eg."If
you say 'Af-Am' like it's some sort of Harvard
hipster lingo shorthand."[DK]

short-handed — (done) without help from
anyone else Eg."Heck, they scored on the
power play goal and shorthanded."[CBC]

single-handedly — without help from anyone
else Eg."Michael single-handedly transformed
the team."[GGL]

single-handed — (done) without help from
anyone else Eg."He sailed single-handed
around the world."[GGL]

sitting on their hands — do nothing Eg."It sucks
that Blago could make an appt., but it's the
fault of the IL legislature for sitting on their
hands and not doing anything to take that
power away from him."[DK]

steady hand in a storm — keeping control of a
situation in a calm and reliable way Eg."The
'steady hand in a storm' argument looks now
to more favor Obama, not McCain."[HP]

sticks hand — to continue doing or using
(something) especially when it is difficult
to do Eg."Conservadems: "Ewww...." sticks
hand into the wrong hole -- and pulls Co-Ops
lever by mistake."[DK]

the hands of — If someone experiences a
particular kind of treatment Eg."A public plan
aims to put care back into the hands of
doctors."[DK]

to hand — pick (something) up and give it to (someone); ~ hold the hand of (someone) in order to help them move in the specified direction Eg."Don't know how much longer I'm going to hand onto Dish."[DK]

to handle — manage (a situation or problem Eg."to handle the task of breaking the sad news to the GOP "[DK]

underhanded — acting or done in a secret or dishonest way Eg."Some clearly believe that the ruthlessness and disregard for ethics and law that Kenney demonstrated in his underhanded defeat of Jean."[CAAB]

upper hand — the position of having power or being in control in a particular situation Eg."who had gained the ratings upper hand during O'Brien's brief "[HP]

hand-fist

open hand - clenched fist — giving freely; ~ generous - a symbol to express unity, strength, or resistance Eg."President Obama held out his open hand as a gesture of his willing to be bipartisan and the Republicans responded with a clenched fist."[DK]

hand-neck

put his hands around the neck — this could be a sign of affection Eg."After seeing a man put his hands around the neck of a fellow customer... "[DMUK]

hand-throat

put his hands around her throat — at some
point she may going to die Eg."then put his
hands around her throat and started choking
her... "[DMUK]

head

a beachhead — an area on a hostile shore
occupied to secure further landing of troops
and supplies; ~ foothold Eg."the state has
emerged as a beachhead for the president's
most aggressive conservative critics... "[PC]

a head-to-head — compete directly with each
other Eg."A head-to-head fight between the
two Republicans "would be a titanic struggle,"
Moore said."[KC]

a straight-ahead — relating to or being music
performed in an unembellished manner
typical of a given Eg."This isn't fair, we know
you, we know that you're a straight-ahead
reporter."[HP]

ahead — farther forward than someone or
something Eg."Whatever happened to the
Obama in campaign mode, always ahead in
the message game? "[DK]

ahead — farther forward than someone or
something Eg."America faces great challenges
in the months and years ahead."[MSN]

ahead of — farther forward than someone or
something Eg."Private health insurers always
manage to stay one step ahead of the
sheriff."[DK]

an empty head — not very intelligent and often do silly things Eg."Mitt Romney, Karl Rove and Sarah Palin. . . an empty suit, an empty heart and an empty head."[DK]

big headaches — emotional stress and depression Eg."Kenney will create big headaches for his pal, Andrew Scheer, even by trying to do this."[CBC]

bobble heads — a foolish, dumb, or ditzy person; ~ a caricature of a famous person Eg."Regardless of whether my rant on corporate-bobble heads rings true with y'all... "[DK]

calm head — an ability to remain calm Eg."Good to see a calm head amongst the "populist" mob mentality diaries flooding this site today."[DK]

clear his head — to stop worrying or thinking about something, or get rid of the effects of Eg."It is a matter of Obama being able to get away and clear his head and re-group."[DK]

clear his head — to stop worrying or thinking about something, or get rid of the effects of Eg."put his troops in peril if someone doesn't clear his head of his romantic ideas about war "[DK]

cloud over the governor's head — a situation or future event that makes you worry or feel unhappy Eg."We're going to have to go back for a special session sometime this fall, and this is going to be a cloud over the governor's head."[NYDC]

cool head — the ability to remain calm and rational during stressful situation Eg. "Earlier, Store said Canada and its polar allies must keep a cool head and work with Russia to solve Arctic disputes." [CAYA]

cool-headed — stay calm in difficult situations Eg. "Just looking at those two men one was a cool-headed Midwesterner." [DK]

dead-headed — dumb, dull, or stupid Eg. "The normally dead-headed House Republican leadership has crafted a platform that can carry the party to victory in November." [DMC]

deer in the headlights — to be so frightened or surprised that you cannot move or think Eg. "She didn't make any huge mistakes and didn't have any "deer in the headlights" moments." [ABC]

ditto heads — an unquestioning supporter of an idea or opinion as expressed by a particular person, organization, etc Eg. "It doesn't matter to her at all that TDS's audience doesn't buy it, as long as the ditto heads do." [DK]

empty head — they are not very intelligent and often do silly things Eg. "Mitt Romney, Karl Rove and Sarah Palin. . . an empty suit, an empty heart and an empty head." [DK]

figureheads — nominal leaders or heads without real power Eg. "A small but influential group of evangelical figureheads acts as if it's brand new information that we can read the heart, instead of an established biblical reality." [FC]

forged ahead — take the lead or make good progress Eg."many other people who rallied around Obama and forged ahead towards a new future "[NEWSY]

get her head — to start to believe something Eg."Using visuals provides enough description to get her head around the discussion."[DK]

go right ahead — if it's ok to do something and you want to say "yes" Eg."But you go right ahead and vote your conscience and kill millions of Americans."[DK]

has a head — to have an ability to understand or deal with (something) Eg."Please watch it, and show it to your friends. Every one of us who has a head, and a heart."[DK]

head — be in the leading position on; ~ give a title or caption to; ~ chief, principal Eg."produce fly-by-night corporations that head for the Third World when they can make more profits there "[TGC]

head back — to begin the act of returning to some place or thing Eg."CBC's Boag said it appears the Conservatives have decided that the only viable solution is Canadians heading back to the polls."[CBC]

head coach — senior coach or manager Eg."Toronto Raptors head coach Nick Nurse shared his thoughts."[CAYA]

head coaching job — coaching or managing at senior level Eg."Prior to accepting the head coaching job, Bjorkgren was a part of the Toronto Raptors."[CAYA]

head down — to hide in order to protect oneself Eg."Though Clinton kept her head down while she mastered her brief as secretary of state—it was the way she took."[NWC]

head hold high — behave proudly, maintain one's dignity Eg."We will go back to our colleagues with our head held high."[TC]

head of — the person in the house who is responsible for making decisions and earning money Eg."Phil Griffin, the head of MSNBC, attributes her success to a certain "magic," and to her application "[NWC]

head out — to leave Eg."but I turn to head out the door with my lit and my lists, and she says "[DK]

head out of sand — to stop avoiding, or trying to avoid, a particular situation by pretending that it does not exist Eg."Get you heads out of the sand."[CAAB]

head scratcher — something that is confusing, mysterious, or hard to understand Eg."This news may have been a bit of a head scratcher for the recipient."[CBC]

head shot of — a bullet or gunshot aimed at the head; ~ a photograph of a person's head Eg."In the ad, which showed up on the lefty Crooks and Liars blog, a standard-issue head shot of the senator "[MN]

head start — an advantage granted or achieved at the beginning of a race, a chase, or a competition Eg."How much of a head start we gave the opposition in defining and characterizing it within the media."[DK]

head to — be in the leading position on; ~ give a title or caption to Eg."With less than one day to go before Albertans head to the polls "[CAAB]

head to head — a conversation, confrontation, or contest between two parties; ~ involving two parties confronting each other; ~ with two parties confronting each other Eg."a head to head contest on jeopardy was held between Governor Sarah Palin and Forrest Gump "[DK]

headed — to proceed or move toward someone or something Eg."not losing sight of where we're headed "[DK]

headed — to proceed or move toward someone or something Eg."Headed for the Old Yeller treatment "[DK]

headed — to proceed or move toward someone or something Eg."The problem we have is with Romney and his sidekick, Paul Ryan, but also where the Republican Party is headed."[DK]

headed — to proceed or move toward someone or something Eg."He woke up late and headed to the pool."[MSN]

headed — to proceed or move toward someone or something Eg."as the clock headed for just four minutes "[NA]

headed back — to begin the act of returning to some place or thing Eg."After the two gave their daughter away, they headed back to their seats."[CAYA]

headed by — having a head of a specified kind
Eg."her campaign — which was headed by Stephen Carter, the same political strategist "[CAYYG]

heading — a direction or bearing Eg."Let's hope this girl is heading straight for the Aloe Vera section."[TBC]

heading — a title at the head of a page or section of a book; ~ a direction or bearing Eg."Jon Stewart will be missed while on vacation, we need him on our team heading into the last quarter."[DK]

heading on over — start moving to a certain destination, a certain way Eg."I'm devastated but every bit counts and this is who we are heading on over."[DK]

heading out — to leave and implies that there is a specific purpose or destination Eg."Obama is heading out for vacation."[DK]

headline — be an important item of news in newspapers or on the radio or television Eg."Bloomberg is juxtaposing their headline with an interview with Tom Daschle."[DK]

headline — be an important item of news in newspapers or on the radio or television Eg."What they are really saying is stated in the column's mocking headline."[DK]

headlines — to be featured on
the headlines of news articles, as due to being particularly important, popular, fashionable, etc Eg."Do health care reform headlines leave you saying "huh?" "[DK]

headlines — to be featured on the headlines of news articles, as due to being particularly important, popular, fashionable, etc Eg."special envoys like George Mitchell and Richard Holbrooke to make headlines "[NWC]

headmaster — the person in charge of a school; ~ the principal Eg."He attempted to scold Obama as if he were the head-master."[DK]

head-on hit — with the head or front making the initial contact; ~ in direct opposition, confrontation, or contradiction Eg."That hit was a head-on hit."[CBC]

headpiece — an illustration or ornamental motif printed at the head of a chapter in a book Eg."That headpiece alone deserves its own paragraph."[TBC]

headquartered — provide (an organization) with headquarters at a specified location Eg."The company is headquartered in Berkeley Heights, New Jersey, United States."[DK]

heads — be in the leading position on Eg."There are heads of nonprofits whose budgets are 5 to 10 times the size of RID that make less than her."[DK]

heads in the sand — to refuse to think about unpleasant facts, although they will have an influence on your situation Eg."I am not crazy, but there are a lot of people with heads in sand and up their ass."[DK]

head-scratching — to show that one is puzzled, doubtful, or uncertain; ~ to show that one has trouble understanding something Eg."her head-scratching response to the question about her Achilles heel "[HP]

headshot — a bullet or gunshot aimed at the head Eg."he was suspended four games for a nasty headshot on "[CBC]

head-to-head — (deal with somebody) in a very direct and determined way, especially in a competition between two people, organizations Eg."professor had already come up with the idea of a head-to-head competition "[DK]

head-to-head — (deal with somebody) in a very direct and determined way, especially in a competition between two people, organizations Eg."She would be going head-to-head with the likes of Ahmadinejad and Kim Jong-il."[DK]

head-to-head — (deal with somebody) in a very direct and determined way, especially in a competition between two people, organizations Eg."She even handled Biden very well on his turf, foreign policy - meeting him head-to-head on every issue, and winning."[DMC]

headwinds — a difficult environment, similar to taking a sailing boat (or in older times, a small ship) against the wind Eg."The Wall Street Journal says its latest polling reveals headwinds for Mitt Romney."[DK]

hit over the head — to describe exactly what is causing a situation or problem Eg."The public often has to be hit over the head."[DK]

hole in the head — emphasizing that you do not want them and that they would only add to the problems that you already have Eg."Liberal Leader Michael Ignatieff says Canadians need another election like a "hole in the head," "[CAYA]

hothead — a person with an excitable, fiery, or impetuous temper or disposition; ~ one who is quick to get angry or act rashly Eg."there's also the little matter of diarrhea-mouth hothead Joe Biden "[HP]

hotheaded — a person with an excitable, fiery, or impetuous temper or disposition; ~ one who is quick to get angry or act rashly Eg."She thought McCain seemed very hot-headed like Bush."[DK]

hotheaded — a person with an excitable, fiery, or impetuous temper or disposition; ~ one who is quick to get angry or act rashly Eg."Inside the White House hotheaded Emanuel may be White House voice of reason."[WP]

in our heads — one is too deeply involved with something or someone Eg."app version of them that we have in our heads after getting to know how they'd react "[DK]

is headed — having a tip, end, or top part of a specified kind Eg."The governor replied that when Putin "rears his head" he is headed for Alaska."[NYTC]

knucklehead — a stupid person Eg."have to take this opportunity to call Ms. McCaughney a Knucklehead McSpasatron of the highest order "[DK]

melon-like head — an idiot, a foolish person Eg."melon-like head yesterday."[DK]

my head and my heart — to do something based on one's own personal desires rather than for pragmatic or practical reasons; ~ let (one's) heart rule (one's) head Eg."But at long last, he had my head and my heart."[DK]

my head and my heart — being hated or killed and being accepted or loved Eg."But at long last, he had my head and my heart."[DK]

my head around — to understand something that is challenging or confusing Eg."I can't get my head around Republicans even knowing what "ethical standards" "[DK]

my head off — talk, laugh, etc unrestrainedly Eg."I was sitting here at the computer, laughing my head off."[DK]

on its head — to misinterpret or misrepresent something so that it is completely incorrect or the opposite of what it should be Eg."Jesus turned the concept on its head by saying how good of a neighbor are you, lawyer."[DK]

on top of my head — you say it without thinking about it much before you speak Eg."I can think of four (previous) repubs off the very top of my head who are die-hard Obama supporters."[DK]

over their heads — when one is too deeply involved with something or someone, or has more difficulties or problems than one can manage Eg."an official they have to deal with, and Gibbs sometimes went over their heads and complained to their bosses "[WP]

overhead — ongoing business expenses not directly attributed to creating a product or service Eg."the insurance company administrative overhead/profits "[DK]

play in head — to manipulate a person in an emotional way Eg."Get Out! playing in my head. Is this one of those moments? This seems big."[DK]

pointy head — a pretentious, self-important intellectual Eg."Betsy Wetsy tells a lie, a volley of tomatoes at her pointy head."[DK]

raced ahead — you're further along or further forward Eg."Over the last 30 years, as its economy has raced ahead "[NWC]

radiohead — an English rock band formed in Abingdon, Oxfordshire, in 1985 Eg."I think if aliens came down from space and killed everybody, they would spare Radiohead."[DK]

rear the head — it starts to appear or be active, often when it had stopped or been hidden for a period Eg."Reared heads reared themselves again at the debate, when she said that Fannie Mae and Freddie Mac "were starting to really kind of rear the head of abuse." "[NYTC]

reared heads — it becomes visible or noticeable Eg."Reared heads reared themselves again at the debate, when she said that Fannie Mae and Freddie Mac "were starting to really kind of rear the head of abuse." "[NYTC]

rears his head — it starts to appear or be active, often when it had stopped or been hidden for a period Eg."The governor replied that when

Putin "rears his head" he is headed for Alaska."[NYTC]

rears his head — he becomes visible or noticeable Eg."The governor replied that when Putin "rears his head" he is headed for Alaska."[NYTC]

rip my head off — to yell at someone or to be ery critical of someone especially very suddenly and without a good reason Eg."I know some of you will have the urge to rip my head off and shit down my neck for speaking against the mob."[DK]

scratching their heads — express puzzlement or perplexity, think hard Eg."A lot of people are scratching their heads over what would cause House Speaker Nancy Pelosi" [NEWSY]

shake my head — to express confusion or bewilderment about something Eg."Just amazing. I shake my head in awe."[DK]

shaking my head — to express disappointment or disbelief in the face of what's perceived as glaringly obvious stupidity or extremely obliviousness Eg."by moving back to Canada and shaking my head in disgust as I cross over the border ..."[DK]

shithead — a contemptible person Eg."because McCain loots like an utter shithead and an idiot right now "[DK]

shoot themselves in the head — to terminate from employment, fire; ~ to express real dislike of something Eg."But he and they are shooting themselves in the head."[CAAB]

spearhead — to serve as leader or leading element of Eg."In the meantime, I'll be helping the fine people at FDL to spearhead an initiative."[DK]

stuck in my head — to be very memorable; ~ to be unlikely to be forgotten Eg."After that I had this tune stuck in my head."[DK]

talking heads — a journalist or pundit, especially one on television, who presents or discusses issues of the day Eg."CNN asking today why none of the high paid talking heads on their networks... "[DK]

talking heads — a journalist or pundit, especially one on television, who presents or discusses issues of the day Eg."why none of the high paid talking heads on their networks could not have ended this "death panel" nonsense "[DK]

talking heads — a journalist or pundit, especially one on television, who presents or discusses issues of the day Eg."All the talking heads claimed to have looked to Walker Cronkite as a role model."[DK]

talking heads — a journalist or pundit, especially one on television, who presents or discusses issues of the day Eg."All the talking heads claimed to have looked to Walker Cronkite as a role model and Jon Stewart put them all to shame, again."[NA]

to head off — to try to stop something from happening Eg."Ask the drug companies to 'volunteer' to negotiate to head off legislation that would make it official."[DK]

turned her head — it has an influence on how that person behaves, especially by making them too proud: Eg."She was quite skeptical about him, but the choice of Biden turned her head."[DK]

whipped his head — more than one can handle; ~ too much Eg."He whipped his head this way and that "[DK]

wiser heads — calm people, thoughts, or actions triumph in the end Eg."Sorry, while I do sympathize with you on your loss, wiser heads in your family should have prevailed."[DK]

wrong-headed — having or showing bad judgment; ~ misguided Eg."Biden won the point, albeit on the Democrats' wrong-headed strategy of a phased withdrawal."[HEC]

Yellowhead — name of a northern Canada city; ~ bird type Eg."Martin Long, the UCP candidate in West Yellowhead, has sociopathic attitudes."[TTC]

head-ass

head up their ass — to be oblivious to the real state of things, from either stupidity or stubbornness Eg."People who think "public" = "bad" just have their head up their ass."[DK]

heads and ass — rude slang to be acting in a way that others deem stupid Eg."I am not crazy, but there are a lot of people with heads in sand and up their ass "[DK]

head-bone

da head bone — a stupid person : numbskull bonehead Eg."It'll take to connect da head bone to da gut bone.Puffy."[DK]

head-butt

headbutted — attack (someone) with a headbutt (an aggressive and forceful thrust with the top of the head into the face or body of another person) Eg."He head-butted Proenza Schouler designer Jack McCollough."[HP]

head-shoulder

stands head and shoulders above — someone or something is much better than others Eg."I think she stands probably head and shoulders above anybody else I can think of "[HP]

heads and shoulders — above other people or things, he, she, or it is a lot better than them Eg."He knows that Jon Stewart is heads and shoulders so much smarter than him."[DK]

heart

after my own heart — someone has likes and dislikes similar to one's own Eg."Now that is a man after my own heart! "[CAYA]

an empty heart — having or showing a lack of feeling or compassion for others Eg."Mitt Romney, Karl Rove and Sarah Palin. . . an empty suit, an empty heart and an empty head."[DK]

at heart — basically bare Eg."they also have the best interests of the American people at heart."[DK]

at the heart of — to be the most important part of something Eg."They lie at the heart of all progressive policies."[DK]

at the heart of — to be the most important part of something Eg."It is hitting at the heart of traditional GOP strongholds."[DK]

beating heart — passionate love, happiness, excitement, and even obsession Eg."South Carolina was the beating heart of the confederacy and its still ticking."[DK]

big heart — a kind and generous disposition Eg."It takes a bog heart and a little ego to do that."[CAYA]

bless her heart — a spoken expression of good wishes, endearment, affection, fondness, sympathy Eg."the latest virtuoso of Frontier Baroque, bless her heart, the governor of the Last Frontier "[NYTC]

bottom of my heart — to express sincere emotions Eg."Sir, from the bottom of my heart, thank you for the obvious caring "[DK]

break heart — express the sadness when someone beloved leaves you inconsolable Eg."That just breaks my heart."[CAAB]

by heart — from memory Eg."What a selfless act, to include the stepfather on such a special occasion, this story warms my heart!! "[CAYA]

by the heart — completely; ~ by memory Eg."We know the truth, not only by the reason, but also by the heart."[DK]

by the heart — completely; ~ by memory Eg."We know the truth, not only by the reason, but also by the heart."[DK]

callous hearts — feeling no emotion; ~ feeling or showing no sympathy for others; ~ indifference to suffering Eg."but these great minds and callous hearts in our American Congress have found others Worldwide more needy then their own citizens "[DK]

capture hearts — to cause another person to feel love for one Eg."Every time Obama said his opponent was right the more surely he captured our hearts."[DK]

cut to the heart — to wound deeply the feelings of; ~ to distress greatly Eg."cut to the heart of what it means to me to be a good person "[DK]

disheartening — causing a person to lose confidence, hope, and energy; ~ discouraging Eg."saying he was bowing out was a little disheartening "[DK]

disheartning — causing someone to lose determination or confidence; ~ discouraging or dispiriting Eg."but it's disheartening to know that so many people are comfortable with it in 20-fucking-10."[DK]

empty heart — having or showing a lack of feeling or compassion for others Eg."Mitt Romney, Karl Rove and Sarah Palin. . . an empty suit, an empty heart and an empty head."[DK]

follow his heart — to act according to one's feelings; ~ to obey one's sympathetic or compassionate inclinations Eg."I believe he sincerely felt embarrassed by his own weakness then, and vowed to himself to do his best to follow his heart."[DK]

for the soft of heart — having feelings of kindness and sympathy for other people Eg."This is not for the soft of heart. It's intense."[NWC]

hard-hearted — incapable of being moved to pity or tenderness; ~ unfeeling Eg."Ryan's wonky persona -- whether you find it refreshing or hard-hearted."[DK]

has a heart — to show kindness and sympathy Eg."Please watch it, and show it to your friends. Every one of us who has a head, and a heart."[DK]

has heart — to have the necessary will, callousness Eg."Barack is intelligent, fiercely so but his intellect has heart."[DK]

heart — to love (someone or something) Eg."I (heart) Oregon vote by mail! "[DK]

heart attack — to be extremely surprised or shocked Eg."I recall my grandmother, born in 1899 having a heart attack in 1967, and because of Medicare she received one of the first pacemakers."[DK]

heart break — to make someone very unhappy, to cause great grief Eg."My heart breaks for this family and any others who are going through the same issues."[CAAB]

heart goes out — feel sorrow or sympathy for Eg."My heart goes out to the family."[CAGLB]

heart of — find or determine the most important or essential facts or meaning Eg."the risky practice at the heart of the financial crisis."[HP]

heart of — find or determine the most important or essential facts or meaning Eg."The financial services sector is the heart of the economy."[DK]

heart of — find or determine the most important or essential facts or meaning Eg."by Dem in the heart of Texas "[DK]

heart of glass — to have or be in a state of extreme emotional fragility or susceptibility Eg."This guy has a heart of glass except when the "needs" of his corporate friends are the issue."[CA]

heart of glass — to have or be in a state of extreme emotional fragility or susceptibility Eg."still wins the "Heart of Glass" award in this election. But you are a great runner-up."[TSC]

heart of the matter — the most important, basic, or fundamental essence or elements of an issue, problem, or matter at hand Eg."There is nothing like comedy to get to the heart of the matter."[DK]

heartbeat — an animating or vital unifying force Eg."If they couldn't profit off of their liberal programming, they'd drop it in a heartbeat."[DK]

heartbreaking tears in mind — expecting sorrow or sadness due to Eg."with the heartbreaking tears in mind (Nearly 11 Million

Cancer Patients Without Health Insurance) "[DK]

heartbroken — to be so sad that it feels like your heart has cracked inside your chest Eg."I'm not. I'm heartbroken."[HP]

heartened — make more cheerful or confident Eg."I was heartened to hear of his commitment to the millions."[MSN]

heartening — increasing cheerfulness or confidence; ~ encouraging Eg."ot over 4,300 views. ...heartening that some Albertans can still read "[CAAB]

heartening — increasing cheerfulness or confidence; ~ encouraging Eg."This heartening explanation from one of our representatives makes no claims to have been the right choice."[DK]

heartening — increasing cheerfulness or confidence; ~ encouraging Eg."John McCain's second visit to Iowa in less than a month is heartening Republicans who say it is proof."[MWC]

heartfelt — (of a feeling or its expression) sincere; ~ deeply and strongly felt Eg."An academic, writes a heartfelt column in support of Rachel Notley and her ND government."[CAAB]

heartfelt — (of a feeling or its expression) sincere; ~ deeply and strongly felt Eg."This was a completely heartfelt and thought out decision."[DK]

heartily — very; ~ to a great degree (especially with reference to personal feelings) Eg."Tell Luke that I am so proud of his decision recommended by and agree heartily with all of his reasons why Obama should be our next president. "[DK]

heartland — the central or most important part of a country, area, or field of activity; ~ the center of support for a belief or movement; ~ the central part of the US; ~ the Midwest Eg."It gives me hope that people in the heartland are seeing that side of Obama."[DK]

heartland — the central or most important part of a country, area, or field of activity; ~ the center of support for a belief or movement; ~ the central part of the US; ~ the Midwest Eg."What a testament to the fact that his connections really are to heartland America."[DK]

heartland — the central or most important part of a country, area, or field of activity; ~ the center of support for a belief or movement; ~ the central part of the US; ~ the Midwest Eg."250 million farmers and others abandoning its impoverished heartland in search of factory work and a better life on the coast."[NWC]

heartless — displaying a complete lack of feeling or consideration Eg."Pricks like Mike Ross aren't just corrupt, they're heartless."[DK]

heartless — displaying a complete lack of feeling or consideration Eg."I wonder how the heartless, merchants of greed feel now. "[DK]

heartless — displaying a complete lack of feeling or consideration Eg."Lukaszuk reminds Albertans that Kenny is heartless and ruthless."[TWT]

heartless — displaying a complete lack of feeling or consideration Eg."He's shown himself to be a contemptible, unfeeling, and heartless human being."[NA]

hearts — the central or innermost part of something; ~ like very much; ~ love Eg."Neglect of our poorer Americans needs enlightened political minds and hearts to view god differently."[DK]

hearts of — that is what you really believe or think Eg."in language that would warm the hearts of neoconservatives (if we had them)"[HP]

heavy hearts — in a sad or miserable state, unhappily Eg."Today, there are heavy hearts across America."[HP]

heavy on hearts — in a sad or miserable state, unhappily Eg."The tragic situation is weighing heavy on the hearts and minds of those"[CAAB]

his heart is not with — someone does not really care about something that they are doing Eg."Don Cherry attempts to contain some of his understandable Boston bias and openly admits his heart is not with the Canucks."[CBC]

hit in the heart — to induce an emotional reaction in someone Eg.“As a step parent this just hits me in the heart... what a wonderful and considerate gesture.”[CAYA]

huge heart — to be kind and generous Eg.“that's wholly absent on the Romney-Ryan ticket: (1) deep knowledge; ~ (2) huge heart and (3) brutal honesty.”[DK]

in her heart — cause someone to fall in love with one Eg.“Even though I am divorced and my adopted daughter no longer has me in her heart.”[CAYA]

in his heart of hearts — that is what you really believe or think, even though it may sometimes seem that you do not Eg.“in his heart of hearts Lieberman has to know he will not fit in with the GOP caucus ”[DK]

in our hearts — that is what you really believe or think, even though it may sometimes seem that you do not Eg.“The country we carry in our hearts is waiting.”[DK]

in our hearts — that is what you really believe or think, even though it may sometimes seem that you do not Eg.“The country we carry in our hearts is waiting.”[DK]

in your heart — that is what you really believe or think, even though it may sometimes seem that you do not Eg.“That's something you just can't fake. Either you have it in your heart or you don't.”[DK]

into the heart — cause someone to fall in love with one Eg."set up their own communications network going into the heart of conservative districts everywhere "[DK]

into the heart of — cause someone to fall in love with one Eg."plunge myself into the heart of the debate now "[DK]

listen heartbeat — very quickly; ~ as soon as is possible Eg."It's something that comes from a place of compassion deep within a person's sacred stillness, to listen to their heartbeat and follow "[DK]

my heart — being accepted or loved Eg."But at long last, he had my head and my heart."[DK]

no heart — to not have the emotional resolve (for something); ~ to be unable to do something Eg."Completely agree and the way to hurt them is in the wallet since they have no heart."[DK]

one with heart — with complete sincerity, devotion; ~ very willingly; ~ with pleasure Eg."He may be a hack, but he's one with heart. Ryan, in contrast, came across as steely cold, "[DK]

open up hearts — to talk in a very open and honest way about one's feelings Eg."what Sarah's calling in this campaign is and will be is to open up hearts of American to give "[RSC]

out of the heart — discouraged Eg."It was a vote out of the heart, and for that you should be commended."[NYTC]

save the heart — you have expressed that you love me, but I don't love you back Eg."I would suggest that those who believe we have to hold our nose and save the heart of the economy reach out to our Congress people and tell them so."[DK]

someone's heart — someone's mind, someone's thinking Eg."Never say you know the last word about any human heart, except maybe Max Baucus."[DK]

sweetheart — denoting an arrangement or agreement reached privately by two sides in an unofficial or illicit way Eg."The White House took plenty of initiative in negotiating a sweetheart deal for Big Pharma."[DK]

sweetheart — denoting an arrangement or agreement reached privately by two sides in an unofficial or illicit way Eg."Are the people who make millions and avoid taxes through havens, dodges, and sweetheart legislatlon."[NA]

take heart — you are telling him to take comfort or take confidence from something Eg."In the meantime, progressives can take heart "[DK]

the heart — to love (someone or something) Eg."The heart will have stopped pumping blood to all extremities of the body economic."[DK]

the heart of — find or determine the most important or essential facts or meaning Eg."The Bruins have been at the heart of such discussions for two straight seasons."[CBC]

the heart of — find or determine the most important or essential facts or meaning Eg."I can find someone getting right to the heart of this lie."[DK]

the hearts — to love (someone or something) Eg."You can't win the hearts and minds of those who have neither."[DK]

the hearts and minds — the intellectual and emotional mindset of the members of some group Eg."You can't win the hearts and minds of those who have neither."[DK]

this cuts to the heart — to say or do something unkind that makes someone feel very upset Eg."All of this cuts to the heart of why I really wanted to become a doctor."[DK]

to the heart — cause someone to fall in love with one Eg."Lou Dobbs is asking someone to assassinate Howard Dean with a stake to the heart."[DK]

touch the hearts — to make them feel empathy or sympathy Eg."I'm sure that it will touch the hearts of each of the IOC members."[BLM]

touched my heart — to make them feel empathy or sympathy Eg."He said the reception Monday from the fans "blew me away" and "touched my heart"."[MSN]

touched the heart — to make them feel empathy or sympathy Eg."what so deeply touched the heart of America and draws people."[RSC]

turn hearts of — you change your opinion or the way you feel about something Eg."She can turn the hearts of people who otherwise would never have considered voting for a Republican."[RSC]

warms my heart — to cause someone to have pleasant feelings of happiness Eg."What a selfless act, to include the stepfather on such a special occasion, this story warms my heart!"[CAYA]

whole-heartedly — with complete sincerity and commitment Eg."They will reason to the right conclusion and support the policy wholeheartedly."[DK]

win the hearts — to gain the love, affection, or admiration of someone Eg."You can't win the hearts and minds of those who have neither."[DK]

win the hearts and the minds — used in reference to emotional and intellectual support or commitment Eg."You can't win the hearts and minds of those who have neither."[DK]

with heartbreaking — causing intense sorrow or distress heartbreaking news; ~ producing an intense emotional reaction or response Eg."with the heartbreaking tears in mind (nearly 11 million cancer patients without health insurance) "[DK]

heartbeat

heartbeat away — causing intense sorrow or distress heartbreaking news; ~ producing an intense emotional reaction or response Eg."multiple cancer survivor heartbeat away from the Presidency "[DK]

heartbeat away — in a position to move into a position immediately upon the absence of one's superior or predecessor Eg. "This woman will be one 72-year-old's heartbeat away from being President of the United States." [HP]

heart-bleed

a bleeding heart — one who shows excessive sympathy for another's misfortune Eg. "Proud to proclaim: I am a bleeding heart Liberal." [DK]

heart-head

an empty heart and an empty head — having or showing a lack of feeling or compassion for others and lacking intelligence or knowledge Eg. "Mitt Romney, Karl Rove and Sarah Palin. . . an empty suit, an empty heart and an empty head." [DK]

heart-mind

heavy on hearts and minds — the intellectual and emotional mindset of the members of some group Eg. "The tragic situation is weighing heavy on the hearts and minds of those " [CAGLB]

heart-soul

heart and soul — doing it with a great deal of enthusiasm and energy Eg."This issue really takes us to the heart and soul of Republican thinking about the wars in Iraq and Afghanistan."[DK]

heel

Achilles heel — a weakness in spite of overall strength, which can lead to downfall Eg."her head-scratching response to the question about her Achilles heel "[HP]

heel-throat

heels on throats —

to be in a position of control or power over someone else;~to have another person in a vulnerable position Eg. "for the very people that have the heels on their throats, convinced that the 'trickle down theory' really explains that smelly yellow 'rain' "[DK]

hide

chaps my hide — to displease or irritate Eg."Believe me...as an Iowan it really chaps my hide."[DK]

hip

shoot from the hip — speak or act recklessly or impulsively Eg."He tends to shoot from the hip and go on gut instinct."[MYDD]

shoot from the hip and go on gut instinct —
speak or act recklessly or impulsively and to trust or follow an intuition or instinct Eg."He tends to shoot from the hip and go on gut instinct."[MYDD]

humane

humane moment — characterized by tenderness, compassion, and sympathy for people and animals, especially for the suffering or distressed Eg."The bride and those present will never forget this humane moment."[CAYA]

jaw

jaws to drop — extremely surprising, impressive, or shocking Eg."The politically progressive communications company formerly known as working assets, has caused some jaws (if not calls) to drop."[MN]

jaw-bone

jawboning — attempt to persuade or pressure by the force of one's position of authority Eg."During the vote, Boehner walked the floor by himself, gently jawboning wavering colleagues when he could."[PC]

knee

at the knee — so nervous or powerfully affected that it is difficult to stand Eg."Unfortunately Harper seems to have learned very well at the knee of his Bush advisors."[DK]

at the knees — so nervous or powerfully affected that it is difficult to stand Eg."Cut them off at the knees, and support progressive candidates directly."[DK]

get down my knees — to beg desperately for something Eg."I get down my knees and pray, we won't get fooled again."[DK]

knee deep — submerged to or reaching as high as the knees; ~ so as to reach or submerge the knees Eg."Pritzker and her failed Chicago based Superior Bank were knee deep in the subprime lending mess."[HP]

knee-jerk — that you respond to something in an equally unthinking way Eg."He may be an arrogantly foolish clown with respect to the knee-jerk winger belief system "[DK]

on knees — to be extremely weak or tired Eg."It is better to die on your feet than to live on your knees."[DK]

take a knee — to publicly protest about something, usually in a situation where other people are standing so that your lowered position is particularly attention-grabbing Eg."And you thought "Taking A Knee" was too much!?! "[TC]

weak in the knees — so nervous or powerfully affected that it is difficult to stand Eg."I got weak in the knees and lost it."[CAYA]

knuckle

bare-knuckled — with no scruples or reservations Eg."a "bare-knuckled" management style that made him easy to dislike "[HP]

laugh

laugh it off — to dismiss something or someone as ridiculous or laughable Eg."although they are tending to laugh it off "[DK]

leg

a leg up — to have an advantage over others Eg."That seniority could give the new Illinois senator a leg up over the others in terms of committee assignments."[HP]

cut the legs — spoil, weaken, or limit somebody's plan or position Eg."It doesn't quite cut the legs out from under the opposition the way some other name would."[DK]

first leg — the first stage or part (of something) Eg."She heard about the horrific quake on the first leg of a trip to Asia."[NWC]

has legs — it will continue for a long time Eg."This has legs, I'm on board."[DK]

has legs — it will continue for a long time Eg."This story has legs regardless of the election results on Tuesday."[CAYYG]

have legs — to have the ability to endure, stay

relevant, or continue to maintain interest Eg."This story can have legs because it hits on so many levels."[DK]

last leg — very tired or near to death; ~ near to the destination Eg."The last leg of Mrs. Obama's Mexico state trip was a sit down discussion with some of Mexico's young leaders and entrepreneurs."[DK]

leggings — tight-fitting stretch pants, protective coverings for the legs Eg."The man has decided to sport wacky leggings and emphasize his beautiful calves! "[TBC]

second leg — the second operation on the same stock - a square-off Eg."The first leg applies to the first operation - a buy or a sell, and the second   leg applies   to the second operation on the same stock - a square-off."[GGL]

the return leg — Each match is called a 'leg' so there is a home leg and an away leg which is sometimes known as the 'return leg' Eg."However, in the return leg in Charlotte, the Mavericks had more than one reason to celebrate... "[CANBA]

limb

on a limb — they do something they strongly believe in even though it is risky or extreme, and is likely to fail or be criticized by other people Eg."I may be going out on a limb."[DK]

out on the limb — they do something they strongly believe in even though it is risky or extreme, and is likely to fail or be criticized by other people Eg."Has the R's out on the limb of the olive branch and he's getting ready to saw them off."[DK]

lung

lunged — to charge or jump at someone or something; to attack someone or something Eg."Instead, Fred Van Vleet lunged with water-bug speed to deflect the ball, securing the win for Toronto."[CTCC]

lungs sounded — as loudly as one can Eg."McCain's lungs sounded shot."[HP]

yelling from the top of our lungs — you shout as loudly as you possibly can Eg."South Carolina's been yelling from the top of our lungs on national politics since this nation."[PC]

man

a man's man — a bit of rough; ~ a man who enjoys men's activities and being with other men Eg."There's a guy with class, a man's man and a heart that cares more... "[CAYA]

dead man walking — someone who is in great trouble and will certainly get punished, lose their job or position, etc, soon Eg."Dead man walking-President Obama's request turns Gov. Paterson into lame duck... "[NYD]

like a man — to suffer, endure, or accept something in a stoic, unemotional manner Eg."It's called acting like a man. Finally."[CAYA]

manly man — man who can make a decision without resorting to an internet poll to help him decide Eg."BHO tries to be a manly man."[RSC]

manly man — man who can make a decision without resorting to an internet poll to help him decide Eg."Tonight, he clearly tried to be manly as he understands manly against Sen. McCain."[RSC]

manly man — man who can make a decision without resorting to an internet poll to help him decide Eg."He's comfortable in his skin and he is a manly man."[RSC]

meat

dog meat — the target of forthcoming violence or ill-will Eg."President Obama knows he is dog meat if he doesn't pass a bill with a public option "[DK]

meat of — a person regarded primarily or solely as an object of sexual attraction or gratification Eg."but the meat of the frame is not in the name "[DK]

meaty — large and having a lot of flesh Eg."To read on the bus tomorrow. Much too meaty for me to absorb in my current, burned out state! "[DK]

red meat — political appeals designed to excite one's core supporters; ~ demagoguery Eg."It's the crazazies of the right wing who just want more red meat, otherwise, I think you're right."[DK]

red meat — political appeals designed to excite one's core supporters; ~ demagoguery Eg."Jason Kenney's policy statements are, by and large, red meat for the angry and uninformed."[FB]

men

straw men — an intentionally misrepresented proposition that is set up because it is easier to defeat than an opponent's real argument; ~ a person regarded as having no substance or integrity Eg."Straw men and knee-jerk attacks are the language of some for God knows what reason."[DK]

mental

mental meltdown — describes a period of extreme mental or emotional stress Eg."if the country somehow has a collective mental meltdown and elects Sarah Palin "[HP]

mind

blow my mind — to strongly affect someone with surprise, wonder, delight, etc Eg."it makes me feel to see Michelle being greeted with warmth and joy as First Lady of the United States. It still blows my mind."[DK]

boggles my mind — something is difficult to imagine or understand Eg."It boggles my mind that the Dems... "[DK]

cast your mind — to think about something that happened in the past, Eg."Cast your mind way back to 2002, halfway through the first Cheney/Bush Jr. administration "[DK]

change his mind — adopt a different opinion or plan Eg."Endorsement will encourage Senator McCain to change his mind."[DK]

change minds — to change one's decision or opinion about something Eg."See if the reality check website has changed their minds."[DK]

change your mind — adopt a different opinion or plan Eg."I hope you change your mind."[DK]

come to mind — (of a thought or idea) occur to someone Eg."What came to mind were public bathrooms."[DK]

do not all mind — saying politely that you will be happy with any of the things offered Eg."Mind you, most of his choices seem unsavoury, as we do not all mind reminding Change Alberta readers... "[CBC]

great minds — a phrase used when one has the same thought or idea as someone else Eg."but these great minds and callous hearts in our American Congress have found others Worldwide more needy then their own citizens "[DK]

have in mind — to be thinking of choosing (someone) for a job, position; ~ to be thinking of doing (something) Eg."I don't think this is what the founding fathers had in mind."[DK]

heavy on minds — to cause someone a lot of worry, concern, or anxiety Eg."The tragic situation is weighing heavy on the hearts and minds of those … "[CAGLB]

high-minded — having strong moral principles Eg."But I actually think those kinds of high-minded statements that often appear in media are not just banal but dishonest."[CBC]

in her mind — her viewpoint, opinion, or belief Eg."and is now shooting the wolves from her own helicopter, in her mind "[DK]

in his mind — his viewpoint, opinion, or belief Eg."the glee in the douche bag's eyes as he was dancing on the President's grave in his mind "[DK]

in mind — to have a plan or intention Eg."with the heartbreaking tears in mind (Nearly 11 Million Cancer Patients Without Health Insurance) "[DK]

in their minds — to someone's feelings or attitude Eg."They have repeatedly brought up plans of other countries, and conservatives won't have any part of "copying" another - in their minds, inferior - country."[DK]

keep in mind — to remember to consider a related idea when thinking about, considering or doing something else Eg."But, it's important to keep in mind, we can't count on more Dems in Congress to get this passed later."[DK]

keep in mind — to remember to consider a
   related idea when thinking about, considering
   or doing something else Eg."But please,
   please, please keep in mind "[DK]

keep in mind — to remember to consider a
   related idea when thinking about, considering
   or doing something else Eg."Please keep in
   mind many Americans generally don't know
   about this issue."[DK]

keep in mind — to remember to consider a
   related idea when thinking about, considering
   or doing something else Eg."Keep in mind that
   Change Alberta is not the NDP."[CAAB]

like-minded — share the same opinions, ideas, or
   interests Eg."MacTavish to land Eakins, a like-
   minded, progressive coach... "[CAYEG]

like-minded — share the same opinions, ideas, or
   interests Eg."conversations with "like minded"
   virtual friends or even total strangers... "[DK]

like-minded — share the same opinions, ideas, or
   interests Eg."and he wants to keep it that way
   before his audience of like-minded people...
   "[DK]

make up mind — to make a decision about
   something; ~ to decide Eg. "dispatching a
   spokesman to say that Burris would have to
   make up his own mind on that... "[HP]

make up their minds — to make a decision
   about something; ~ to decide Eg."Many said
   they were waiting for the debates to help
   them make up their minds for good."[DK]

mens' minds — have as many minds (or opinions) as you have people Eg."Our... constitutional heritage rebels at the thought of giving government the power to control men's minds."[DK]

mind — used to highlight or emphasize an exception, qualification, or explanation Eg."People need to mind their business and stop thinking they know what is best for people."[DMUK]

mind numbing — excessively boring, tedious, or dull; ~ repetitive; ~ of an activity Eg."Framing is the newest term for mind numbing propaganda."[DK]

mind you — someone must consider or pay attention to a particular piece of information Eg."Mind you, the party is slick."[CAYEG]

mind you — someone must consider or pay attention to a particular piece of information Eg."Mind you, most of his choices seem unsavoury, as we do not all mind reminding Change Alberta readers."[CBC]

mind you — someone must consider or pay attention to a particular piece of information Eg."sure we'd have ferocious internal debates about foreign policy--debates which, mind you, are clearly over Sarah Palin's head..."[DK]

mind you — someone must consider or pay attention to a particular piece of information Eg."Mind you, I'm not saying Palin's not stupid enough to yank her kids out of school "[DK]

mind-blowing — to strongly affect someone with surprise, wonder, delight, Eg."President Obama gave at least $10 that would be around $600,000,000 and at a $100 each it would be mind-blowing."[DK]

mind-boggling — having a very powerful or overwhelming effect on the mind Eg."His weighing in on a mind-boggling swath of governmental and political activity "[WP]

mindful — deliberately aware of your body, mind, and feelings in the present moment, in order to create a feeling of calm Eg."Be mindful of your wellness."[TC]

mind-fuck — something that is extremely confusing or mind-boggling Eg."The participants believed they were getting medical care because they were in a medical study. That's a murderous mindfuck."[DK]

mindless — stupid and meaning nothing Eg."Banning a bot does not prevent them from just spewing out more mindless messages from other sites."[CA]

mindless — stupid and meaning nothing Eg."First of all, he is the poster boy for the fanatical, mindless, angry far right."[DK]

minds — used to highlight or emphasize an exception, qualification, or explanation Eg."You can't win the hearts and minds of those who have neither."[DK]

never mind — not to worry about something, not to trouble yourself, it doesn't matter Eg."I've got whiplash from the conflicting statements coming out this week. Oh never mind."[DK]

not mind — to suggest that one is making the statement in an unwilling way Eg."He doesn't mind breaking the law as he showed with his TFW program! "[CAAB]

not mind — to suggest that one is making the statement in an unwilling way Eg."Rahm Emanuel, a fiery partisan who doesn't mind breaking glass and hurting feelings.."[DK]

open mind — a mind receptive to different opinions and ideas Eg."He is trying to keep an open mind."[DK]

open mind — a mind receptive to different opinions and ideas Eg."An open mind means searching for facts, not ignoring them in the interest of fairness."[DK]

open minded — willing to consider ideas and opinions that are new or different to your own Eg."of course reality, and open minded consideration of events, occurs on this site."[DK]

open minded — willing to consider ideas and opinions that are new or different to your own Eg."But I have no idea what to expect in the meet. I'm going in open minded."[MSN]

our minds — to think often about someone or something; ~ to be obsessed with someone or something Eg."Half measures won't reinstate his integrity in our minds at this point."[DK]

our minds — to think often about someone or something; ~ to be obsessed with someone or something Eg."We use our minds, unlike the robots on the right."[DK]

out of my mind — unable to behave or deal with things normally Eg."I'd be hooked on drugs so bad trying to find peace I'd be outta my mind with spiritual misery."[DK]

over someone's head — beyond someone's ability to understand; ~ without someone's knowledge or involvement, especially when they have a right to it Eg."Sure we'd have ferocious internal debates about foreign policy--debates which, mind you, are clearly over Sarah Palin's head."[DK]

over the mind — the leading or controlling mind in a group mind Eg."I have sworn upon the altar of God, eternal hostility against every form of tyranny over the mind of man - Thomas Jefferson."[DK]

political minds — interested in the way power is achieved and used in a country or society Eg."Neglect of our poorer Americans needs enlightened political minds and hearts to view God differently."[DK]

sharp-minded — to be able to understand or grasp information quickly Eg."don't thoroughly control, especially where he might be pitted against any sharp-minded, well-prepared opponents "[DK]

simple-minded — does not have the ability to use reason and understand Eg."News media sites are saturated with simple-minded bot messages."[CA]

small minded — having or showing rigid opinions or a narrow outlook Eg."Maybe Alberta is just too small (or small-minded) for you."[CAGLB]

speak his mind — express one's feelings or opinions frankly Eg."the wisest man in the court, with the most freedom to speak his mind, and the least credibility "[DK]

speaking his mind — to say what one thinks : to state one's opinion Eg."Joe Lieberman has never been shy about speaking his mind."[HP]

state of mind — a person's emotional state : mood Eg."I think this action in your current state of mind is not rational."[DK]

that in mind — while thinking about someone or something Eg."With that in mind, I have compiled a handy resource for your perusal."[DK]

unlike minds — a capability network whose associates are at the leading edge of social change thinking Eg."Have political conversations with undecided and especially competing or unlike minds."[DK]

mind-ears

mind and ears closed — to willfully ignore or refuse to listen to something or what someone is saying Eg."Mind and ears closed, screw the taxpayers is his posture."[OC]

mouth

big mouth — who speak a lot, be loquacious, often nosily or boastfully Eg."He's just a jerk. A debutante, status quo asshole with a big mouth and an ego to match."[DK]

big mouth — who speak a lot, be loquacious, often nosily or boastfully Eg."Your opposition can edit into devastating 30 or 60 second spots that will make you look, well, look like a big mouth talk show host."[PC]

both sides of their mouths — you say different and contradictory things to different people Eg."They talk out of both sides of their mouths depending upon how the wind is blowing."[DK]

diarrhea-mouth — a tendency speak constantly or at length without thinking Eg."there's also the little matter of diarrhea-mouth hothead Joe Biden "[HP]

diarrhea-mouth hothead — not intelligent and a person who is impetuous or who easily becomes angry and violent Eg. "there's also the little matter of diarrhea-mouth hothead Joe Biden "[HP]

foaming at the mouth — to produce foam from the mouth because of illness or excitement Eg. "whether these foaming at the mouth imbeciles represented anyone other than themselves, speculation "[DK]

foul-mouthed — using or characterized by a great deal of bad language Eg."foul-mouthed hockey-jock son-in-laws and other household dramas "[HP]

in my mouth — to suggest that someone said or meant something that he or she did not actually say or mean Eg."Ooops, I just threw up a little in my mouth."[DK]

lying mouth — to sound artificial or contradictory Eg."Ian Patton [cop] he and his lying mouth arrived in Alberta as a drop-out from a religious college in San Francisco."[CAAB]

mouth shut — to not discuss or mention something Eg."He'd kept his damned mouth shut."[DK]

mouth the words — to say what someone else was just going to say Eg."DSCC and DCCC and towards progressive candidates who will stand on principle rather than just mouth the words and phone it in."[DK]

mouthing off — to talk in a loud, unpleasant, or rude way Eg."The law is very clear…just another Conservative mouthing off."[CAAB]

mouthpiece — an official spokesperson for someone or something; ~ someone who speaks or answers questions on behalf of someone else Eg."I worked as a government mouthpiece for a number of years, but I got sick of having to spin the truth to line up with their narrative."[GGL]

mush mouthed — a person who speaks indistinctly or inarticulately Eg."Being mush-mouthed helped give the patrician Bushes the common touch."[NYTC]

open mouth — with the mouth open, as in surprise or excitement Eg."Don't worry, the minute he opens his mouth, we are going to hit him up styles! "[DK]

out of her mouth — anticipate what someone is about to say; ~ also, completely agree with someone Eg."Don't even get me started on the stuff that came out of her mouth."[DK]

pen to mouth — used as a comfort device, are a substitute for the original breast, cigarette Eg."I pray ...from Ebert's pen to Obama's mouth."[DK]

rose to the mouths — the passion and the drama that is tango -- striking, really Eg."They created buzzwords and pithy sound bites that rose to the mouths of their elected "leaders"."[DK]

shut mouth — used to tell someone in a rude way to stop talking She angrily told him to shut his mouth Eg."Bayh is smart to keep his mouth shut."[DK]

side of mouths — to give completely different advice or opinions about something in different situations Eg."Leaders who speak about health care out of both sides of their mouths."[DK]

muscle

flexing their muscles — to try to worry an opponent or enemy by publicly showing military, political, or financial power Eg."Republicans in Congress may be playing a high-risk game by flexing their muscles."[REU]

muscle-taxing — intensity of the exercise is high enough that physiological adaptation must occur Eg."This was listening as an aerobic exercise, muscle-taxing and calorie-burning."[DK]

nail

tough as nails — strong and very determined Eg."She's tough as nails, and that can be hard for some people."[PC]

naked

naked truth — plain unadorned facts, without concealment or embellishment Eg."Artists bring us the naked truth."[DK]

neck

bottle-necked — a situation that stops a process or activity from progressing Eg."That information is bottle-necked over here in Europe in the European media."[DK]

hang around your neck — your responsibility and it causes you a lot of worry Eg."If knowledge hangs around your neck like pearls, instead of chains, you are a lucky man... Alan Price."[DK]

lying neck — to assume or expose oneself to some risk, danger, or responsibility; ~ to imperil oneself or lay oneself in harm's way; ~ to risk damaging one's reputation Eg."I have been waiting for her to grab them by their lying necks."[DK]

neck and neck — even in a race, competition, or comparison Eg."Obama is now the world's biggest celebrity, just after Angelina and Brad.

I guess they're neck and neck right now."[CAYA]

shit down my neck — disapproving to stay close to someone, watching everything that they do Eg."I know some of you will have the urge to rip my head off and shit down my neck for speaking against the mob."[DK]

wring its neck — used to say that one is very angry with someone Eg."We wring its neck and takes the precious!!! "[HP]

nerve

having the nerve — you are criticizing them for doing something which you feel they had no right to do Eg."for having the nerve to be so smart and enjoy culture "[DK]

lost his nerve — become frightened or timid, lose courage Eg."The former Navy pilot must have lost his nerve somewhere along the line."[HP]

lot of nerve — they show great rudeness; ~ a lot of audacity or brashness Eg."This widow-peaked pipsqueak to my side has a lot of nerve."[DK]

my nerves — they annoy or irritate you Eg."Your diary and others like it calm my nerves."[DK]

nervous — having or showing feelings of being worried and afraid about what might happen Eg."Thanks for this I'm so nervous knowing how Gore & Kerry managed to screw it up."[DK]

the nerve — an exclamation of shocked disapproval regarding something someone said or did Eg."She had the nerve to challenge Stewart."[DK]

noise

noise — to be very outspoken about something, especially that which one dislikes or disagrees with Eg."Good job, hitting on the issues rather than the noise."[DK]

noisy — to have a tendency or habit of speaking incessantly, indiscreetly, and/or in a noisy, boastful manner Eg."It's hard to see how she benefits from her noisy point of view."[DK]

nose

hardnosed — being tough, stubborn, or uncompromising; ~ hardheaded sense; ~ tough-minded Eg."and on through the hard-nosed views she developed as a senator, like voting to authorize the Iraq War... "[NWC]

hold their nose — to do something unpleasant or something we don't really want to do Eg."It was the thing that will make them hold their nose and vote for the Cons! "[CAAB]

hold your nose — to do something unpleasant or something we don't really want to do Eg."I told him that his options were to either "step-aside" (meaning abstain) or "hold your nose" (secret ballot vote for a Democrat)."[DK]

look down his nose — to think of or treat (someone or something) as unimportant or not worthy of respect Eg."He really does look down his nose at the rest of us."[NA]

our nose — take a chance and follow our nose Eg."I would suggest that those who believe we have to hold our nose and save the heart of the economy reach out to our Congress people and tell them so."[DK]

snot-nosed (punk) — overly conceited or arrogant Eg."Listen you snot-nosed punk" would have been his preferred response several times."[RSC]

stick someone's nose — to involve oneself in an intrusive or nosy manner into something that is not one's business or responsibility Eg."It certainly wasn't up to us here in Europe to stick our noses in too much."[DK]

sticking nose — to get involved in or want information about (something that does not concern one) Eg."When are you intolerant tyrants going to stop sticking your noses in other people's business? "[MSN]

through his nose — to pay too much money for something Eg."Personally shove his committee gavel up his ass and pull it out through his nose."[DK]

through the nose — to pay too much money for something Eg."those of us paying through the nose for private health care with outrageous deductibles and covering only 80% of any bill "[DK]

up your nose — that they annoy you Eg."If you can't afford a boat, and are standing tiptoe in the water, the rising tide goes up your nose. Barney Frank" [DK]

wrinkled-nose — to show surprise, uncertainty, or disgust at something Eg."Oh, please. She broke out the wrinkled-nose flirty bit again."[DK]

nut

nuts — crazy; ~ manic or eccentric; ~ out of one's mind Eg."Uh oh, Palin's gonna find herself with a pair of Biden's nuts hanging off her chin come Thursday night."[DK]

person

first person memory — you see the event from the same visual perspective that you originally did Eg."Now a generation later the ones who still have first person memories are now well into their 80's."[DK]

rib

rock-ribbed — resolute or uncompromising, especially with respect to political allegiance; ~ (of landscape) characterized or dominated by rock formations; ~ craggy Eg."expanding the tent with a cosmopolitan, progressive tack, instead of trying to lure rock-ribbed conservative traditionalists "[CAYEG]

ribbing — good-natured teasing Eg."I can also count on some good-natured ribbing from the folks who call me "that Democrat!"."[DK]

sense

my sense — the ability to perceive; ~ a sense of warmth; ~ a mental perception or awareness Eg."My sense is that all of the people who were here today, or at least most of them if not all, would be very loyal to our present MP, Beaudoin said."[CAYA]

sex

sexy — exciting; ~ appealing Eg."It's not sexy but it's got teeth: Report a Glenn Beck incident to the FCC."[DK]

shit

shit — a contemptible or worthless person; ~ tease or try to deceive (someone); ~ an exclamation of disgust, anger, or annoyance Eg."I guess free spirit means you can make up any shit you want."[DK]

shit-eating — smug; ~ self-satisfied Eg."Despite their shit-eating grins, Democratic leaders nearly got rolled today."[DK]

shithole

shithole — an extremely dirty, shabby, or otherwise unpleasant place Eg."I hate people in this shit hole city."[TC]

shoulder

cold shoulder — a show of intentional unfriendliness; ~ reject or be deliberately unfriendly to Eg."She also said Arctic states Sweden, Finland and Iceland were similarly concerned they were given the cold shoulder."[CAYA]

off my shoulders — no longer have to worry about something or deal with something difficult Eg."It was a huge shock to me so it just kind of took a weight off my shoulders."[NEWSY]

on someone's shoulder — being something that is someone's to deal with Eg."John, wait up," called Sen. John Kerry, D-Mass., clapping a big hand on John McCain's shoulder."[HP]

shouldered — to push or thrust with; ~ be, stand, act Eg."He shouldered most of the blame."[CBC]

shouldered — to push or thrust with; ~ be, stand, act Eg."Much of the blame for the overreaction has been shouldered by Clinton communications boss."[CBS]

sight

short sighted — nearsighted; ~ lacking imagination or foresight Eg."The book is a collection of the many short-sighted and out-of-touch claims made in recent years."[DK]

skeleton

skeletons — to have (an) embarrassing, unpleasant, damaging, or incriminating secret(s) from one's past Eg."The longer the primary goes on, the more time there will be to find some more skeletons on Mitt Romney."[FC]

skin

comfortable in his skin — relaxed and confident in one's manner of presenting oneself and interacting with others Eg."But I always mean what I say," Biden said, totally comfortable in his skin. And so does Romney."[DK]
in his skin — relaxed and confident in one's manner of presenting oneself and interacting with others Eg."He's comfortable in his skin and he is a manly man."[RSC]

save his own skin — to protect yourself from danger or difficulty, without trying to help other people Eg."He has done this simply to save his own skin."[CBC]

skin color — color of skin which is complexly determined Eg."supportive of people of all sexual orientations, and supportive of peaceful people of all religious beliefs and skin colours... "[CBC]

skin deep — superficial as opposed to the substance Eg."Other than that, Palin's grasp fluctuated between wafer thin and skin deep."[HP]

skin guru — expert on skin beauty related matters Eg."Mud may sound like it doesn't belong on the face, but any skin guru will tell you to think again! "[TBC]

skin in the game — a situation in which high-ranking insiders use their own money to buy stock in the company they are running Eg."Account Manager at BDC says it's important to show you have some skin in the game."[CABDC]

skin in the game — a situation in which high-ranking insiders use their own money to buy stock in the company they are running Eg."The investors wanted Tony to have some "skin in the game," so he had to raise $25,000 to purchase a stake in the factory."[NEWSY]

skinny — (of an article of clothing) tight-fitting; ~ a skinny person; ~ a pair of skinny pants, especially jeans Eg."The world was introduced to this skinny kid from Chicago with the funny name and sticky-outy ears as a candidate for POTUS."[DK]

thinner the skin — to be very sensitive, easily insulted and unable to deal with anything that might be seen as criticism Eg."Then it only stands to reason that the thicker the bone, the thinner the skin, no? "[DK]

thin-skin — overly sensitive to criticism; ~ quick to take offence; ~ irritable; ~ touchy Eg."He was, in many ways, a perfect partner for Armando/Big Tent democrat, who shares his thin skin, self-involvement, and humorlessness."[DK]

thin-skinned — overly sensitive to criticism; ~ quick to take offence; ~ irritable; ~ touchy Eg."Yet Iran's thin-skinned regime apparently remained deeply suspicious."[TOUK]

under his skin — to irritate or upset someone; ~ to affect someone positively even though he or she does not want or expect to be affected that way Eg."Obama clearly got under McCain's skin."[HP]

wafer thin and skin deep — very thin; ~ (especially of a margin of victory) very slim; ~ barely achieved and superficial as opposed to the substance Eg."Other than that, Palin's grasp fluctuated between wafer thin and skin deep."[HP]

skull

broken skulls — skull, head fractured due to beating in the fight Eg."hard fought for Labor laws of Canada, earned through broken skulls and bitter strikes of our workers in the past "[CAYA]

inside of her skull — to be heavily intoxicated by drugs or alcohol Eg."into a comfortable fantasy that it was literally burning the inside of her skull... "[DK]

death-skull — dry smile when pain, death is expected Eg."The two just stood stiffly facing the audience with death- skull grins on their faces."[HP]

smell

old man smell — the specific chemical that gives
old folks their unique odor, scientists suspect,
is a compound called nonenal Eg."That "mean
old man" smell will linger on the chairs."[DK]

soul

soul-less — lack human qualities and the ability to
feel or produce deep feelings Eg."Bill Maher
was right when he called them "soul-less cash
whores"."[DK]

spine

chills down my spine — to make someone feel
very frightened Eg."The email I received today
sent chills down my spine and is further proof
that..."[DK]

grow a spine — develop some courage Eg."It
seems Nancy Pelosi has grown a spine."[DK]

spine of jelly — a cowardly act (has no spine like
jellyfish) Eg."when we need someone who's
spine isn't made of jelly... "[DK]

spineless — to have no backbone, meaning
unable to stand erect, upright, to be forceful
or direct in word or action Eg."When
negotiating, you shouldn't be totally
spineless."[DK]

spineless — to have no backbone, meaning
unable to stand erect, upright, to be forceful
or direct in word or action Eg."When people
on this site have criticized the Democratic

Congressional leadership as "spineless" during
my time on this site."[DK]

spineless — to have no backbone, meaning
unable to stand erect, upright, to be forceful
or direct in word or action Eg."I agree that
Harry Reid is a spineless, gutless idiot."[DK]

stiff-spined — inflexible, and it sounds positive
Eg."I don't see anything Kucinich got by being
stiff-spined."[DK]

spine-gut

spineless, gutless — a timorous, insipid, or
apprehensive person; ~ someone without
conviction, confidence, or courage Eg."I agree
that Harry Reid is a spineless, gutless
idiot."[DK]

spit

spit in the bucket — something is utterly
worthless Eg."But that spit in the bucket
seems even smaller when the UCP plans to
cut overall health spending."[YEG]

stomach

feeling my stomach — to feel nervous or anxious
Eg."I felt a sinking feeling in my stomach that
something wasn't quite right."[DK]

had the stomach for a fight — to not feel brave
or determined enough to do something
unpleasant Eg."He wore down Hillary Clinton
and wiped out John McCain, so we knew he
had the stomach for a fight."[DMUK]

has no stomach — to not feel brave or determined enough to do something unpleasant Eg. "and a sign that the industry has no stomach for another war of words with a president "[HP]

have butterflies in the stomach — feeling very nervous Eg."At the beginning of an exam, I always have butterflies in my stomach."[GGL]

my stomach can — to feel nervous or anxious Eg."I don't know if my stomach can take more."[DK]

punched in the stomach — something that affects you strongly in an emotional sense Eg."He could deliver a harsh message, but do it with a little sense of humor, so you'd feel punched in the stomach but not in the face."[WP]

sick to my stomach — feeling very disgusted or angry Eg."It all made me a little sick to my stomach."[CAAB]

stomach it — unable to tolerate someone due to an aversion or a strong sense of disgust or dislike for them Eg."I could not stomach it."[DK]

stomach-turning — to make someone feel sick, often because they are angry or upset about something Eg."Wine and ice cream? My stomach is turning at the thought of that combo."[DK]

stomach-turning — to make someone feel sick, often because they are angry or upset about something Eg."Stomach-turning photos show animals caught In oil spill."[HP]

stronger stomach — the ability to not be
bothered by things that many people find
disgusting, shocking, or offensive Eg."You
would have to have a much stronger stomach
in the romance department to end things like
that."[HP]

stomach-face

punched in the stomach but not in the face —
something that makes you feel very upset or
disappointed , especially when you have
been trying hard to achieve something Eg."He
could deliver a harsh message, but do it with a
little sense of humor, so you'd feel punched in
the stomach but not in the face."[WP]

tail

tailspin — lose emotional control, collapse, panic
Eg."If we have to rename it now to pull
ourselves out of any perceived tailspin."[DK]

my tail off — to work very hard Eg."I've got to
take it from here and work my tail off."[CAYA]

tail — follow and observe (someone) closely,
especially in secret; ~   provide with a tail
Eg."But it could easily be the tail end of a
piece on the economy or taxes or some wing
nut rant."[DK]

tail end of — the last or hindmost part of
something Eg."Caught the tail end of this
interview with a right-wing conservative radio
host."[DK]

tailgate — to follow so closely behind a vehicle that a collision is very likely or inevitable Eg."Don't tailgate me then get pissy when I do it back."[TC]

tears

happy tears — experience emotions so intense they become unmanageable Eg."That made me cry instantly, happy tears."[CAYA]

tears — a sudden showing or burst of intense energy or activity; ~ a spree, binge, or indulgence of intense or prolonged alcohol consumption Eg."with the heartbreaking tears in mind (Nearly 11 Million Cancer Patients Without Health Insurance) "[DK]

teeth

clenched teeth — internalize ones's anger; ~ you squeeze your teeth together firmly, usually because you are angry or upset Eg."there were lots of clinched teeth moments for McCain "[RSC]

cutting his teeth — get one's first experience by doing, or learn early in lif Eg."after cutting his teeth on KO's show, maybe he's ready for the Daily Show??? "[DK]

falling into the teeth — person treats you badly and unfairly Eg."His mistake was falling into the teeth of fame and privilege."[MSN]

gnashing of teeth — to show one is angry, upset, etc Eg."You can hear the gnashing of teeth from John Kerry."[NYTC]

got teeth — got enough power or support of authority to compel obedience or punish offenders Eg."It's not sexy but it's got teeth: Report a Glenn Beck incident to the FCC."[DK]

has its teeth — to have enough power or support of authority to compel obedience or punish offenders Eg."The media has its teeth into what it has them into."[DK]

lying through his teeth — to say something completely untrue Eg."He knows that he is lying through his teeth to voters."[CBC]

teeth whistling — a whistling sound can occur when a patient says a word with an "s" in it Eg."I totally agree it is old man teeth whistling."[HP]

toothless — lacking genuine force or effectiveness Eg."The safeguards in the bailout bill are toothless."[DK]

testosterone

testosterone-fuelled — energized or caused by the thing specified Eg."Kenney thinks he can speed that up with a testosterone-fuelled "war" with the feds and British Columbia."[CAAB]

throat

clearing his throat — to make a noise in the throat for attention Eg. "the one who commands every room he walks into, who can silence a strategy session just by clearing his throat "[NWC]

jump down his throat — to respond angrily to someone Eg."Please jump down his throat when he does or says something stupid! "[CAAB]

jumps down sb throat — to respond angrily to someone Eg."And McCain jumps down Couric's throat instead of letting Palin answer."[DK]

ram anyone's throat — to force someone to accept something unpleasant Eg."don't try to ram their ideology down anyone's throat... "[DK]

thumb

big fat thumb — someone making a mistake when they are typing or deciding Eg."all whilst his big fat thumb blocks any increases in the minimum wage... "[CAAB]

rule of thumb — a broadly accurate guide or principle, based on experience or practice rather than theory Eg."a good rule of thumb is that it should cover 20% to 30% of the purchase price... "[CABDC]

rule of thumb — a broadly accurate guide or principle, based on experience or practice rather than theory Eg."the rule of thumb on these late hits is... "[CBC]

thumb down — an indication of rejection or failure Eg."Please sign in to rate a Thumb Down! "[CAYA]

thumb up — give an approval Eg."Please sign in to rate a Thumb Up! "[CAYA]

thumb-nose

thumb to nose — to show very clearly that one does not like or care about (something Eg."U.S. Sen. Joe Lieberman was in the news last week for applying thumb to nose at former Democratic..."[MN]

toe

frozen toes — apprehension or doubt strong enough to prevent a planned course of action a loss or lack of courage or confidence; ~ an onset of uncertainty or fear Eg."how much you kept giving and how you kept on going, even with frozen toes "[NEWSY]

keep on the toes — they cause you to remain alert and ready for anything that might happen Eg."It's up to "us" to keep these folks on their toes and make them fight for what "we" won."[DK]

on a level toe to toe — directly opposing or competing with each other Eg."on a level toe to toe..."[NA]

tips of my toes — someone or something that keeps you on your toes forces you to continue directing all your attention and energy to what you are doing Eg."to the tips of my toes...what a guy..he reads and does his homework... "[DK]

to toe a line — either to conform to a rule or standard, or to stand poised at the starting line in a footrace Eg."So Clinton had to toe the liberal line in order to round up the votes he needed to pass his programs in the Congress."[DMC]

to toe his line — either to conform to a rule or standard, or to stand poised at the starting line in a footrace Eg."Any emp or contractor stupid enough to toe his line should go with him."[OC]

toe to toe — (of two people) standing directly in front of one another, especially in order to fight or argue Eg."Obama has to go toe to toe with John McCain" [RSC]

toes

toe-to-toe — (of two people) standing directly in front of one another, especially in order to fight or argue Eg."They have to be outsmarted, since the media's rightward slant cannot be beaten toe-to-toe."[DK]

toe-to-toe — (of two people) standing directly in front of one another, especially in order to fight or argue Eg."Gibbs's aggressive side was on public display last month when he went toe-to-toe with Sean Hannity."[WP]

tongue

a tongue-in-cheek — a humorous or sarcastic statement expressed in a mock serious manner Eg."I'm guessing that working assets means this as a tongue-in-cheek joke."[MN]

holding my tongue — you do not say anything even though you might want to or be expected to, because it is the wrong time to say it Eg."My successes come from holding my tongue now, restraint of tongue and pen."[DK]

restraint of tongue — keeping once thoughts to oneself, so you don't say something you will regret! Eg."My successes come from holding my tongue now, restraint of tongue and pen."[DK]

sharp-tongued — (of a person) given to using cutting, harsh, or critical language Eg."Emanuel, the fiercely competitive and sharp-tongued Chicagoan... "[MSN]

speaking in tongues — it is a practice in which people utter words or speech-like sounds, often thought by believers to be languages unknown to the speaker Eg."While most people will be watching Thursday's VP debate to find out whether Sarah Palin will start speaking in tongues... "[HP]

spoke in tongues — is a practice in which people utter words or speech-like sounds, often thought by believers to be languages unknown to the speaker Eg."At Sarah Palin's old church in Wasilla, they spoke in tongues."[NYTC]

tongue action — to kiss each other or use the tongue in a constantly and wild way Eg."tongue action-like a snake. He's physically revolting."[HP]

tongue-cheek

tongue-in-cheek — in an ironic, flippant, or insincere way Eg."Tongue-in-cheek, he described the Republican's own nonexistent health care plan perfectly."[DK]

tongue-in-cheek — in an ironic, flippant, or insincere way Eg."perhaps tongue-in-cheek welcoming her endorsement of their prize bill "[DK]

touch

out of touch — lacking in awareness or sympathy Eg."The book is a collection of the many short-sighted and out-of-touch claims made in recent years."[DK]

veins

deep in the veins of — means you feel so deeply for a person that they have become a part of you feel them through every part of you Eg."Support for Helena Guergis runs deep in the veins of true blue Tories in her riding."[CAYA]

voice

public voice — as any style or tone that has a chance of persuading any other people (outside of one's intimate circle) about shared matters, issues, or problems Eg."Oppress people because of their gender, sexuality, race, or social class are effectively anti-Canadian and do not deserve a public voice."[CAAB]

wrist

a slap on the wrist — a mild reprimand or punishment Eg."I don't like that Joe made it out of yesterday with a slap on the wrist."[DK]